Poetics of Dislocation

Meena Alexander

Poetics of Dislocation

THE UNIVERSITY OF MICHIGAN PRESS

Ann Arbor

Copyright © by the University of Michigan 2009
All rights reserved
Published in the United States of America by
The University of Michigan Press
Manufactured in the United States of America
⊗ Printed on acid-free paper

2012   2011   2010   2009   4   3   2   1

A CIP catalog record for this book is available from the British Library.

Library of Congress Cataloging-in-Publication Data

Alexander, Meena, 1951–
    Poetics of dislocation / Meena Alexander.
      p. cm. — (Poets on poetry)
    ISBN 978-0-472-07076-3 (cloth : alk. paper)
    ISBN 978-0-472-05076-5 (pbk. : alk. paper)
    1. Poetics.   I. Title.

PN1031.A43   2010
808.1—dc22   2009033065

On the other hand rasa is something that one cannot dream of expressing by the literal sense. It does not fall within workaday expression. It is, rather, of a form that must be tasted by an act of blissful relishing on the part of a delicate mind through the stimulation of previously deposited memory elements which are in keeping with the vibhavas and anubhavas, beautiful because of their appeal to the heart, which are transmitted by [suggestive] words [of the poet]. The suggesting of such a sense is called rasadhvani and is found to operate only in poetry.

  This, in the strict sense of the word, is the soul of poetry.

—Abhinavagupta, *Locana* (ca. 1000 CE)

Contents

III. Migrant Memory

IV. Poetics of Dislocation

V. In Conversation

Paper Boat (Preface)

It was a cold day in late February. The winds gathered force. Sleet covered the streets, though by late afternoon there was some relief. The stout stone building that housed us kept us from the elements, though it had clearly been hard for the members of the audience, mostly students, to make their way to the lounge where we gathered. The event involved a public conversation focusing on a new book of poetry I had just published. A friend and colleague sat across from me at the table and asked me about the raw materials of poetry, the process of composition, migration, and invisible workings of memory. When our back-and-forth ended, the questions came.

One made me lean forward and squint a little, almost as if what was being asked was something the dim light prevented me from seeing. The questioner was alluding to something that had come up earlier: the drifts of paper that emerge as part of the writing process.

"If you took the papers that you have all over your desk, papers you have written on and set aside, if you put them together and decided to make a house, what sort of house would it be?"

I looked at him squarely.

"A boat."

"What kind of house," he repeated. "I mean what sort of house would you make?"

"I wouldn't make a house."

"No?" He looked surprised.

"I would make a boat, the kind of boat that's like a tent. You take a piece of paper and fold it to make a square, then turn it into a conical hat, a tent, a boat."

He let me go on.

"It would have to float," I said to him. "That's essential. Though I could settle for a tent."

Later I thought to myself, if I have to settle for a tent, it should have a guy rope tethered to a cloud.

A floating tent.

A tent for a poet who finds it hard to be securely in place.

I have lived here in these dense, canyon-ridden, subway-gouged streets longer than anywhere else in the world. But in memory I often see a seascape, green-gold, darkening into indigo. I spent a good part of my childhood crossing the waters that join the west coast of India to the east coast of Africa. At the age of eighteen I went to study in England. I returned to India and, in some restlessness I am hard put to name, left again to come to New York City.

But stout brushstrokes, broad swaths of geography, what sense do they make in terms of the texture of poetry?

And what might home mean to such a poet?

Where does she search for it? What does she stumble upon? Where does she belong? And what of the cosmopolitan ideal of community that is not bound by the stringencies of one particular place?

These are some of the questions I ask myself in the reflections that follow.

O so many questions. Sometimes, even in dreams, I don't know how to hold my tongue.

The tension between cosmopolitanism and regionalism is not new in the history of literary culture. In classical Indian poetry, the idea of place is powerful, and poets who write in a regional language, an outcrop as it were of place, are thought to partake of the *desha-bhasha* (language of the native place). Balanced against this is the notion of a cosmopolitan language, part of *marga*, the Great Way, allowing for a poetry that can be read and written in disparate places.[1]

Given that globalization, with all its fraught complications, is a vivid reality, it makes sense to ask how English, a world language, works for an immigrant poet who lives in New York City.

I ask this as a woman who grew up with several languages,

someone whose notion of locality edges into dream, a phenomenology of the everyday hard to square with the watertight notions of selfhood and cultural belonging that nationalism seeks
to enforce. Indeed the idea of American poetry with its rich
genealogies was something that I had to teach myself to struggle
with and through.

In his manuscript papers, some of which are collected and
translated now, Walter Benjamin evokes a necessary way of thinking about truth, a "harmonic concept of truth which we must acquire so that the false quality of watertightness that characterizes
its delusion [vanishes]. . . . The truth is not watertight. Much that
we expect to find in it slips through the net."[2]

It seems to me that Benjamin's notion of a slipping, pulsat-
ing, musical truth sits well with a sense of American poetry as a
living fabric connected by affective threads to other geographies, other histories, other languages, other ways of naming
the sun and the moon.

After all, nothing could be more vital than the poetry of a
great northern continent that has opened its arms to the restless, throbbing life coursing through its borders.

NOTES

Some of these thoughts first emerged at the discussion mentioned
above on February 22, 2008, at the Friday Forum, Ph.D. program in
English, CUNY Graduate Center: "On the publication of *Quickly Changing River:* Meena Alexander in conversation with Wayne Koestenbaum."

1. For a brilliant elaboration of this, see Sheldon Pollock, "Cosmopolitan and Vernacular in History," in *Cosmopolitanism,* ed. Carol A.
Breckenridge, Sheldon Pollock, Homi K. Bhabha, and Dipesh Chakra-
barty (Durham, NC: Duke University Press, 2002), 15–53.

2. Walter Benjamin, Ms. 502, *Walter Benjamin's Archive: Images, Texts,
Signs,* trans. Esther Leslie, ed. Ursula Marx, Gudrun Schwarz, Michael
Schwarz, and Erdmut Wizisla (New York: Verso, 2007), 71.

I. Poetry and Place

Home Ground and Borderlands

1.

The new American poet thinks in many tongues, all of which flow into the English she uses: a language that blossoms for her. Places stick to her and with them histories, strands of local knowledge. She is aware of violence and warfare, she has experienced multiple dislocations, not uncommon now in our shared world.

She has read Emerson. She is exhilarated by what it might mean to think *history is an impertinence and an injury*. She loves the notion of self-reliance, which she translates as self-invention, and she is haunted by the truth of her experience, where injury might be caused quite precisely by the forgetting of history.

On a clear night in northern Colorado, she stares out at the Rocky Mountains. The moon is floating above bruised rocks. It pierces her, a sudden sense, words compacted in her brain as if in response to a question. She hears herself respond aloud to no one in particular:

We have poetry, so we do not die of history.

She does not know what she means by this, but she hears the sounds of the night: a horse neighing, crickets, a passing truck. No other human voices reach her ears. She carries the moment in her memory.

Later, back in the metropolis where she has lived as an immigrant for more than half her life, she finds a book tucked away on a shelf. It's a paperback with blue covers, with an image of blossoming clouds on the front, a book of prose reflections composed by a man, a Palestinian poet. She comes upon a sentence that pierces her to the quick:

> For here, where we are is the tent for wandering meanings and words gone astray and the orphaned light, scattered and banished from the center.[1]

She realizes that these words, composed in another place, in another language, words written in a time of war, translate well.

Where she is, migrant memory pitches its tent.

This is her home ground, this borderland of desire and meaning making. No elsewhere.

2.

Contemporary American poetry exists in a vital mesh of filiation. The international movements of migration and settlement in the United States, as well as the existence of internal exiles, those who feel displaced as minorities within their own land, have created a pulsing, throbbing net of meanings within which the poet can exist, within which she tries to make sense.

The writings of the poet Édouard Glissant are of cardinal importance here and relevant to much more than just the cultural context of the Carribean. In *Poetics of Relation,* after a sustained reflection on the Middle Passage, he writes of "his continuous / discontinuous thing: the panic of the new land, the haunting of the former land." For Glissant, even as *errantry,* the migrant possibility of existence, is foremost, the notion of *relation* as he spells it out gathers power. It implies not foreignness, not what is rendered Other, but rather what is shared and as such can enter into the intricate exchanges of self-identity and the making of poetry.

Glissant writes: "The power to experience the shock of elsewhere is what distinguishes the poet." The poet draws his sustenance from Elsewhere. Poets who were born, or lived in "the Elsewhere" enter into the explosive network of *relation,* a notion, partly mystical, stitching up the erasures that Otherness might enforce. In his discussion of the "rooted errantry" of St.

John Perse, Glissant speaks of the paradox of a memory that is continually returning to an impossible place: "What in fact is this always vanishing memory? What is this place (this house) the one they always say we come from?"

But out of this painful reckoning come the shining strands of a poetry constantly slipping in and out of place, a lyric movement that undoes the teleology of narrative and where "the explosion of the instant obliterates duration."[2]

While Glissant speaks of "chaos" or fractal parts, the sociologist Zygmunt Bauman evokes the flow of a "liquid modernity." He argues that any given map of the world dependent on national and regional borders only goes so far in making sense of an era when the anchorages of place and community dissolve, when travel across borders—linguistic, cultural, and state borders—becomes not an aberration but the norm. It seems to Bauman that the power of the Internet with its continuously shifting virtuality only hastens the dissolution of these other previously fixed borders.

With this melting away of an older order come new ways of thinking about identity. "One becomes aware," writes Bauman, "that 'belonging' and 'identity' are not cut in rock, are not secured by a lifelong guarantee, that they are eminently negotiable and revocable." He argues that the very notion of identity is born out of "a crisis of belonging."[3]

What becomes of the nation, one might ask, in such a reckoning—the space modernity has taught us to belong to? After all, we are all marked by the passports we carry or the papers we are not permitted to carry. One can easily be put into detention if the body or its identifying papers seem to merit such treatment at the hands of the authorities. And in terms of identity, surely one could argue versions of such a crisis have been with us for a very long time. There is nothing new in exile. It is as ancient as the notion of home.

In *Kadambari*, a classic of seventh-century Sanskrit literature, a melancholy king asks a caged parrot: "Who are you? How did you come here? How were you caught in this cage?" The parrot's narrative turns on the question of his own metamorphic identity. To be a person is to be subject to change, to endure changes in places around you and changes in one's own substance. We are born in a place and so too we die. Mortality lies at the end, the final knot that prevents us from slipping off the rope of common sense.

Yet there is much to learn from this notion of a liquid life. In a new century there are ways of being and knowing that the seventh-century parrot would have had to use his magical intuitive powers to experience.

But how does memory work with and through these shifting valencies of time and place? The question is important for those who are concerned with the reading and writing of poems.

In *The Art of Memory,* the great scholar of the Renaissance Frances Yates begins with a reflection on Cicero's *De Oratore.* She tells us how the poet Simonides of Ceos was able to remember the precise places at which guests at a banquet were seated. The banquet hall suddenly collapsed, but the poet who was miraculously called out was able to return and identify the missing, naming the dead so their relatives could claim them for burial.

Poetry in place as a powerful elegiac force, a functional force in our shared world, and memory as sheer aftermath . . . the tale of Simonides makes us think of this. For Cicero, the art of memory was essential and stood as a guiding force both for life and for rhetoric. For memory to work, clear arrangement was essential: the arrangement of place.

> He inferred that persons desiring to train this faculty (of memory) must select places and form mental images of the things they wish to remember and store those images in the places, so that the order of the places will preserve the order of the things.[4]

What happens, we might ask, when we confront the loss of place so that, rather than following through to the order of things preserved in memory, the rupture of place forces us to confront the radical dislocation of things, images, even sensations?

What happens when the internal map of place is torn, when what we are faced with are not fixed settlements but pinhole scatterings, dismemberments, a "line of flight," several lines of flight?[5] I draw the potent phrase from the reflections of Deleuze and Guattari, that mad, utterly brilliant philosopher-couple, the two speaking here as it were in one breath.

My mind moves to the idea of cyberspace. How to make sense of Cicero's mnemonic—the order of places securing the order of things—in a world that faces the plethora of postings in cyberspace?

In order to enter that zone we must finally let go of the embodied distances that place grants. But what does this do to what we commonly think of as the past?

I think of cyberspace, which is no place at all, as akin to the dark imaginary out of which poems come, their rhythms, their discrete music punctuating the inner life.

And perhaps even more persistent for me is the way in which the flashing up of disembodied messages provides a curious fit with my migratory life.

The life I have lived is lost to me when I travel to another town or city. I have to learn a new way of dressing, of figuring out buses and cabs and trains, of fronting the world.

The table where I once sat to write, the window out of which I gazed, the tea or the glass of wine I enjoyed, all this is cast aside in a newness without hold, and all that I am seems poised precariously at the rim of a future which has come into being quite precisely by undercutting the past. So memory becomes virtuality: other lives, other places lived in, a shimmering backstory to a radically unstable present.

We are faced with at least two ways of touching the past. One ties us with silken bonds to the densities of ordinary life. The other chops and scatters our identity in the air, bits and pieces capable of ceaseless rearrangement.

In our lives, as in our poems, we need to play both rhythms, stitch ourselves into history through two kinds of music, one and the other coming together to reveal the ordinary densities of our lives as well as the curving lines of our poems, lines that live in a space underwritten by the imagination, *cire perdue* to the sensorium of our days.

There are many different ways of thinking about place, and even in the life of a single poet the sense that she or he makes of the hold of place can change quite sharply.

In his essay "The Place of Writing," Seamus Heaney evokes the way in which poets have traditionally been thought to embody the spirit of the place so that place seems to find voice through its poet.

Reading him, one thinks of Rabindranath Tagore in Santiniketan, Yeats in Ballylee, and Robinson Jeffers in Carmel, all poets whose work might be said to incarnate the spirit of place. But to think of the bond between poetry and place as inevitable would be to naturalize what is in effect a poetic strategy, a deliberate reaching out, ways in which a poet might draw on structures and details of landscape, custom, and ceremony that a place affords.

Heaney speaks of a "filial relationship with region" in the early work of Yeats. He argues that the elements of landscape, both physical and emotional, enter into the poem, granting it a distinctive power. He contrasts this with a radically different relationship the poet might have with place. His example is the late Yeats, a poet whose concerns have changed and for whom the poem itself provides "a verifying force" with landscape becoming nothing more or less than the zone of the poem's coming to ground: its realization. Heaney writes of Yeats's tower in Thoor Ballylee, a building that allowed the poet to establish "an outpost of poetic reality in the shape of a physical landmark." Here he argues "poems have created a country of the mind, rather than the other way round (and the more usual way), where the country has created the mind which in turn creates the poems."

And of Yeats and his tower, a presence both iconic and real that entered so forcefully into the creation of this major poetry, Heaney writes: "Here he was in the place of writing."[6]

The statement is all the more powerful for its simple brevity. A poet might spend a lifetime entire, it seems to me, or even several lifetimes, and never be there in that: the place of writing.

Yet this way of thinking of poetry and place also begs a question. What of poets whose lives have taken difficult routes where the return to a loved place long held in memory is difficult or even impossible, where place itself has altered beyond recognition such that to return, even in memory, involves a certain violence, a disturbance not easily endured?

In such cases one needs to reflect on a poet who is cast out of place rather than securely in place, a poet who must reckon with radical dislocation, whose roots are as imaginary as the routes she or he has traveled are actual and visceral. And in saying this I do not in any way mean to say that the roots such a poet might claim exist only in the mind as pure fabrication. Rather that they too, like much else in the working life of a poet, even while drawing on the body and its expressive powers, on the mind and memory, have to be precariously invented.

Agha Shahid Ali, the Kashmiri-American poet, has a poem called "Evanescence." It draws overtly on Emily Dickinson and her brilliant jagged circuits of space, but the voice is all his own as Ali invents his own America, a geography of dissonance, place tearing open to reveal another place, an elsewhere the poet must claim in order to reach where he wants to go:

> When on Route 80 in Ohio
> I came across an exit
> to Calcutta
>
> the temptation to write a poem
> led me past the exit
> so I could say
>
> India always exists
> off the turnpikes
> of America
>
> so I could say
> I did take the exit
> and crossed Howrah . . .

This splitting and seaming of place, shredding in order to reconstitute the spatial geography of America, is one of the characteristics of the poets I am specially interested in: poets whose memories intrude into what one might think of the ordinary extension of everyday lives, forging through the tokens of loss, a culture of belonging.

Elsewhere, Ali evokes solitude, a recurring note that sets the stamp on perception, language attuned to the singularity of the isolate individual:

> You didn't throw away
>   addresses from which
>   streets
>
> departed. There's
>   no one you know
>   in this world.[7]

In his last book, published just before his own untimely death, Ali turns to his mother's death in America and the transport of her body to Kashmir for burial, a trajectory so exquisitely painful that the poems overflow with images that keep marking mortality's final border. Yet it is through this elsewhere that meaning comes. The last poem, "I Dream I am at the Ghat of the Only World," sets up a living theater for beloved others who have crossed the waters of death. We hear the imagined voices of Eqbal Ahmed and James Merrill, both friends of the poet, summoning presences who bring that other country ever closer now, its harmony of voices that slip and slide into each other, a necessary overture to the making of poems. Ali evokes a houseboat in Kashmir next to an "island of burnt Chinars." But miraculously that landscape opens onto another: a country in the north, and a house in Amherst:

> But the trees have vanished when I step off the boat,
> Instead there is a house, the one in Amherst, the one
> where my mother fought death, by heart able to quote—
>
> to the last from the Urdu of Ghalib, from the Persian
> of Hafiz . . .[8]

In the end, the cadences of poetry are what we hold onto as we approach that dark elsewhere just beyond our own palpable sensual realm. This is Shahid's gift to us: a knowledge bought dear by a poet of exquisite form.

The poet A. K. Ramanujan spent much of his adult life in the United States. He lived in Chicago, and the urban settings of that bustling, violent city entered into the jeweled precision of his work, the miniature landscapes of his passion. Loss of place runs like a bloody thread through his writing and with it the phantom force of forgetting. In "Looking for a Cousin on a Swing," the speaker turns to childhood; the memory of a girl cousin on a swing; desire that sways back and forth between a boy and a girl; and how in later life, in exile from childhood, the grown woman keeps searching for that very tree:

> Now she looks for the swing
> in cities with fifteen suburbs
> and tries to be innocent about it
>
> not only on the crotch of a tree
> that looked as if it would burst
> under every leaf
> into a brood of scarlet figs
>
> if someone suddenly sneezed.

Desire, plucked from dislocation and loss, drives the self. What is lost becomes the impossible object, source of both poetry and memory. In "No Amnesiac King," Ramanujan picks up the story of Sakuntala, the heroine of Kalidasa's celebrated play, a lovely woman forgotten by the king who had married her. The king himself is struck by forgetfulness so that the beloved is lost to him, exiled in a forest, till out of the belly of a fish comes the ring that had slipped off Sakuntala's finger and the king, startled into recognition, finds the whole sullied past flowing back. But the poet is not like that. There is no magic shock that can restore the forgotten world, no trembling screen to be torn till the voice miraculously recovers:

> One knows by now one is no amnesiac
> king, whatever mother may say or child believe.
>
> One cannot wait any more in the back
> of one's mind for that conspiracy
>
> of three fishermen and a palace cook
> . . . .
> and recover at one stroke all lost memory.

What exists is an intricate composition of parts sifted through longing and necessity, a self made up of the worlds that brought it into being—family, cities, the natural hold of things, and desire that uncouples the mind from certitude and in that feverish process allows the poem to come into being.

In a poem called "Saturdays," memory is layered onto the landscape and ancestry onto the body of the fitful other, summoning the future forward. The body itself is viewed as "an almanac," a multicolored map that is intrinsic to the worlds that have beckoned it into being:

> two cherry trees,
> Chicago's four November leaves,
>
> the sulphuric sky now a salmon pink,
> the wife's always clear face
> now dark with unspent
> panic, with no third eye . . .

The elements that compose self and place are in constant motion and make for a fitful inconstancy, and consciousness spreads itself as air might or water. Ancient India and its palimpsests of knowledge flow into the wet streets of Chicago with its bus stops, x-ray machines, bank tellers, laundromats, all of it elemental to a self that takes its inspiration both from the Bhakti poetry of medieval India and from Whitman's "Song of Myself":

> lion faces, crabs for claws,
>   clotted on their shadows
> under the stone-eyed
>
> goddesses of dance, mere pillars,
>   moving as nothing on earth
> can move—
>
> I pass through them
>   as they pass through me
> taking and leaving
>   . . . .
> and even as I add,
>   I lose, decompose

into my elements,

into other names and forms,
past and passing . . . [9]

Such mottled, hybrid identities take multiple forms in Ramanujan's writing. He looks back at his own father, an astronomer
and mathematician, who believed in astrology and Newtonian
physics. He reveals how his father's chosen clothing was part of
the complex colonial world in which he was immersed, an elegant bricolage that both bore the weight and revealed the poise
of a culturally mixed identity:

> He wore neat white turbans, a Sri Vaisnava caste mark (in his
> earlier pictures a diamond earring), yet wore Tootal ties, Kro-
> mentz buttons and collar studs, and donned English serge
> jackets over his muslin dhotis, which he wore draped in tra-
> ditional brahman style. He often wore tartan patterned socks
> and silent well-polished leather shoes when he went to the
> university, but he carefully took them off before he entered
> the inner quarters of the house. [10]

What does it mean for his father to wear such clothing in the
years before and after Indian independence? The question is
important when facing Ramanujan's brilliant speculations on
Indian languages, the nature of folklore, and the ways in which
the taxonomies of classical Tamil poetry allow for iconic landscapes—spaces that convey the need of the soul.

The answer reflects back on the son. The father's landscape
is an India which exists now only as it is held in imagination, for
all around is the complicated sometimes dark terrain of the new
world, a world of brittle endings, of ferocious newness. And it is
in this new world that the poet's crystalline reflections on classical Tamil poetry unfold.

In the book of translations *The Interior Landscape,* Ramanujan
reveals how in classical Tamil poetry, the perfect placement of an
image, the evocation of a tree, seashore, or flower can reveal the
speaker's state of the soul. Landscape can be either inner (*akam*)
or outer (*puram*). The poems of the *akam* or inner landscape
evoke love, desire, loss, while poems of the outer world have to

do with events in public space, wars, kings, elegies for dead heroes. There are five specific landscapes for love in *akam* poetry and each "place," each *paysage état d'âme,* has attached to it a flower, a season, a bird, a beast, a kind of water (whether flowing or not), that conveys a predominant emotion. These emotions range from the joy of sexual union to the anxiety of separation.

In these classical poems place becomes a theater for the soul, with the lover's emotions set at the heart of the enterprise. The landscape of inwardness becomes the anchorage of desire, mysterious in its utter force:

> Bigger than earth, certainly,
> higher than the sky,
> more unfathomable than the waters
> is this love for this man
> of the mountain slopes
> where bees make rich honey
> from the flowers of the kurunci
> that has black stalks.
>
> (Tevakulattar. Kur 3.)[11]

From a first-century poem in Tamil, its symbolic landscape held in the intricate taxonomy granted desire, we move into a zone of crisscrossing histories, cartographies of desire that threaten to leave one stranded, memories that have no obvious sheltering hold.

Time has a special valency in postcolonial thought—it is the time of violation and the time of redemption, the wound of history laid bare through the task of memory. But can the structures of language sustain a memory that cuts through disparate places, bodies, tongues? Can words crystallize the abyssal past?

It is the genius of Derek Walcott that he is able to take the landscape of his native Carribean and imbue it with the coruscating texture he needs for his poetic meditations. The landscape he creates is both magisterial and scarred, multiply forged by the riches of European civilization and the brutal histories of colonialism and slavery. Walcott uses the intricate structures of English poetic forms as well as the vibrant twang of island patois. A transformative power is everywhere evident.

In "The Schooner Flight" his persona Shabine is a man at home only on the wild seas, utterly dislocated, forced to invent himself:

> I'm just a red nigger who love the sea,
> I had a sound colonial education,
> I have Dutch, nigger and English in me,
> and either I'm nobody, or I'm a nation.[12]

Later we see the pain and yes, the glory this entails, when Shabine, cast out from the republic he thought was his, says: "I had no nation now but the imagination."

In his Nobel lecture "Antilles: Fragments of Epic Memory," Walcott writes of the fragmented cultures and languages that have entered into his life and his art.

> Break a vase, and the love that reassembles the fragments is stronger than the love which took its symmetry for granted when it was whole. The glue that fits the pieces is the sealing of its original shape. It is such a love that reassembles our African and Asiatic fragments, the cracked heirlooms whose restoration shows its white scars. This gathering of broken pieces is the care and pain of the Antilles, and if the pieces are disparate, ill fitting, they contain more pain than their original sculpture, those icons and sacred vessels taken for granted in their ancestral places. . . . And this is the exact process of the making of poetry.[13]

The perfection of poetry emerges from the piecing together of shattered parts, ferocious and necessary translation. Walter Benjamin's celebrated essay "The Task of the Translator" works an undersong to Walcott's thinking. But while for Benjamin "a real translation is transparent; it does not cover the original, does not block its light," for Walcott something else is at work. The fragments of a vessel that Benjamin evokes, glued together so that the seams of glue are invisible and the mystic perfection of "the pure language" shines through, gives way in Walcott's reckoning to the broken, glittering beckoning of lives and languages adrift in the new world, a world that poetry must both bear witness to and celebrate.[14]

In the long autobiographical poem "Another Life" filled with Wordsworthian echoes, Walcott turns to an alphabet of stars, plucked from his island home. He invokes classical figures from myth, incarnated as the commonest of black folk, penurious, forced into lives that offer them no escape:

> Ityn! Tin! Tin!
>> From Philomene, the bird-brained idiot girl,
>> eyes skittering as the sea-swallow
>> since her rape,
>> laying on lust, in her unspeakable tongue,
>> her silent curse.

The "idiot girl," like others around her, exists in a landscape of the poet's creation. Indeed the act of painting, of layering and spreading paint on canvas, becomes iconic, a signal of the mind in the struggle to make sense. The great poet is also an accomplished painter of landscapes, and the dense accumulation of paint on canvas allows him a way of figuring out the complexities of ontology. Taking on the voice, the vision of van Gogh writing to his brother, his beloved other—Theo—the speaker takes us into the heart of the mystery. As the apostle Paul knew, what grants vision also burns and consumes. The entry into the chaos of the cosmos is part and parcel with the entry into history. Creativity lies bedded in the unrest of rock and root and tree and human soul.

> The eyes sweat, small fires gnaw
> at the edge of the canvas . . .
> . . . .
> Remember Vincent, saint
> of all sunstroke. . .
> . . . .
> Dear Theo, I shall go mad . . .
> Nature is a fire,
> through the door of this landscape
> I have entered a furnace.

There is no escape from the fires of existence. Life itself unfolds. It is in this way that the notion of "another life" Walcott evokes time and again takes on a dark power. For the post-colonial poet the "master" is always absent and the "pages of the sea" lead him to molten, metamorphic material, genealogic ore, rife with violation. His mixed-race origin brings history unutterably close to the child, a "thin / tortured child" who longs for erasure.

> I searched the sea-wrack for a sea-coin:
> my white grandfather's face,
> I heard in the black howl of cannon,
> sea-agape,
> my black grandfather's voice . . .
>
> I hoped for your sea-voices
> to hiss from my hand,
> for the sea to erase
> those names a thin,
> tortured child, kneeling, wrote
> on his slate of wet sand.[15]

Here, as in Wordsworth's *Prelude,* another long poem of childhood and the growth of the imagination, the child is father to the man. But Walcott's vision takes him far afield from the soil and stones of a small, secluded place. Pastoral implodes. Imagination forces the poet to truths that ordinary life could not easily support. "There is a memory of imagination in literature," writes Walcott, "that has nothing to do with actual experience and is in fact another life." Rupturing the amnesia of the slave, this power is tied up with the "awe of the numinous, the elemental privilege of naming the New World which annihilates history."[16]

But history is annihilated only so it can be resurrected on the page and turned into a mirror of the fractured, teeming soul. An extraordinary cavalcade of poetry comes into being: through the force of adult imagination, the poet who began as a divided child forces together precisely what would tear him apart. In this way the poem itself provides a shelter for the homeless mind.

For the Sri Lankan poet Jean Arasanayagam, born in 1930, the same year as Walcott, born like him on an island, but on the other side of the planet, home is where the haunting starts.

Like Walcott, she is a painter as well as a writer and her landscapes are clotted, dense forms, filled with tiny details of color and texture and sense, within which violence is bedded. Arasanayagam's poetry written during the ongoing civil war in Sri Lanka, is replete with ghostly presences, mothers, fathers, grandparents, young children, boy soldiers. Family is encrypted in the darkening landscape, even as body and soul are torn by shifting ethnic borders.

The freedom of the writer, after all, consists in being part of history, being bloodied by it yet able to breathe free air. But how does one enter history?

Jean Arasanayagam was born into a Dutch Burgher family in Jaffna. She married a Tamil and in the violent ethnic upheavals of the island nation she found herself forced to seek shelter in a refugee camp. Her poetry, which was deeply personal and marked by images of gardens, peaceable landscapes, transforms into a torn, bewildering space, a violent zone of eruptions, barely habitable. Bit by bit we realize how a poetry of witness emerges. Indeed this was borne in on me, quite powerfully, hearing Arasanayagam read her war poems a few years ago at the Interlit festival in Erlangen, Germany.

In a long, meditative poem "Passages" she muses on what joy might mean in a time of bloodshed:

> That was no time to mourn, then how do we remember
> Joy, only a single thread snarled between the
> Interstices of those ruined pillars
> Leaves its brilliant silk caught between
> The edge of teeth that bite on memory[17]

The familiar landscape shifts under her gaze. The old notions of belonging have to be discarded forever. In the notes for a talk given at a British Council gathering, Arasanayagam writes with great perception about the how her inner life and the violent world come together:

> The landscape was unmarred until 1971. . . . The river over which the white kokas flew now had bodies which casually drifted down river—the bodies of the insurgents of 1971.

Even here, I was the watcher on the hills, untouched virtually by what was happening around me.

With the events of 1977–1983 I found myself moving into history and becoming part of it. . . . I began to explore my own identity—the really serious question began to arise: "Who was I? Identity meant Race—my racial identity. I write endlessly on this theme—the colonial inheritance—and the landscape keeps changing, changing all the time."[18]

There is no elsewhere to flee to, no other country. "I have no country now but self," the poet writes, in what seems to us now an anguished variant of Shabine's wild cry. The imagination must take up residence on earth, in the tense present, even as place becomes aftermath:

> We talk as if it is another country
> The harsh rock of flesh hacked with hatchets
> The secret men with masks who belong to bloodnights
> The death carvers, but no blade is delicate enough
> To chisel something that gives like moss
> What adheres can be scraped off with fingernails

It is the task of the poet to enter into the violent present—"Someone has to wipe the blades clean / Remove the smell of old blood."[19]

3.

In the United States the writer and performance artist Anna Deveare Smith has entered boldly into the terrain of ethnic violence. For Smith, ethnicity defined as where one comes from, becomes the portal through which we enter the realm of shared existence. For her, the gaps between places, and with those gaps, the fissures of everyday language constitute the defining feature of American experience. In her introduction to *Fires in the Mirror* Smith muses on "American character." In order to catch the pitch of American character, the peculiar tension that constitutes it, she traveled all over the country listening to people, gathering words, the tone and rhythm of voices. "There is an inevitable tension in America," she writes:

It is the tension of identity in motion. . . . Can we guide that tension so that it is in fact, identity in motion, identity which like a train can pick up passengers and take them to their destination? Or is this tension always going to be derailed onto a sidewalk where some innocents are waiting to get struck down.[20]

It is no accident that the work as a whole was conceived in the aftermath to the bloody riots that exploded in Crown Heights, Brooklyn, after one black child, Gavin Cato, was killed by a car in a rabbi's motorcade, and another badly injured. In retaliation a Jewish rabbinical student was stabbed to death. He died in the same hospital as the child Gavin Cato.

For Smith, language becomes a bearer of tension and it is in the breakdown of syntax that she discovers the "multiple symphonies" she is searching for. The differences of cultural origin, the circumstances of birth become key to the shifting and often fraught negotiation of what a self might be. And a sense of place is critical to this. Place becomes the outer rim, as it were, to the bodily self, a necessary anchorage shot through with breaks, contradictions in meaning making that reveal the polyphonic nature of what the culture is. For Smith there is no other way to make sense of America. She writes:

Many people do remark on the circumstances of their "cultural" birth, their original nationality, their ethnicity. American character is alive inside of syntactical breaks. . . . My sense is that American character lives not in one place or the other, but in the gaps between the places, and in our struggle to be together in our differences.[21]

The journey inward, marking the "gaps between the places," is poignantly revealed in the experimental prose text *Dictée* by Theresa Hak Kyung Cha, a poet and video maker who was born a year after midcentury. She died tragically in 1982, killed in the basement of her New York city apartment. In her text, languages are constantly unraveling under the pressures of coming to voice, coming to visibility in a partitioned homeland, in a time of postcolonial exile. Syntax falls short of sense. The voice comes to rest in a temporality marked by perpetual aftermath.

Memory succors itself on a traumatic returns. The tongue is bitten and starts to break.

The visceral physicality of Cha's presentation consists not in going out of one's own skin and entering the body of the Other—the hallmark of Smith's empathic method. Rather, Cha's method is to give voice to the divided self, a self rendered alien by the force of memory. And it is here that the labor of language begins, the task of healing. Hence the importance of the trope of the tongue in her writing, the organ that makes for speech, a speech marked by the demands of a culture struggling to exist in the aftermath of colonialism:

> Bite the tongue. Between the teeth. Swallow
> deep. Deeper. Swallow. Again, even more.
> Until there would be no more organ.
> No organ. Anymore.
> Cries.
>
> Bit by bit. Commas, periods, the
> pauses. Before and after.
> After having been. All.
> Before having been.[22]

The gaps between the places are borne on the tongue, within the memory of a single body. Cha's homeland, Korea, is partitioned and she is forced to learn two colonial languages, French and English, in order to survive. Mourning the death of her mother, Cha seeks to measure the spaces in the soul mourning makes. To seek out the sources of self is to discover a broken language that not even memory can contain.

What Anna Deveare Smith was to call "the tension of identity in motion" is acted out by Cha in words whose provenance are elusive, a torn tongue that paradoxically forces us back into history.

The energy and daring of American letters are embodied in such performative acts, that of Smith on stage, drawing on the turmoil of public space, Cha's on the page and on the video screen where the body lays itself open, its senses choreographed to a text of many parts, a dance of survival.

I think it is of such survival that the poet Joy Harjo writes in her poem "A Map to the Next World":

> You will see the red cliffs. They are the heart, contain the
>   ladder.
> A white deer will greet you when the last human climbs
>   from the destruction[23]

For Joy Harjo the dispossession of her Native peoples becomes the blood-soaked thread that runs through her poetry. Her job is to make a map tough enough and delicate enough for the wandering soul. In "A Map to the Next World" she writes of the mystical power of the poet as mapmaker, of the spiritual light needed to read the warnings we are given. What human beings need is passage through multiple worlds, and myth must be brought in to help. We need horses, white buffalo, deer, all the delicate creatures that stand for grace and power. The destruction of nature and of Native homelands warns us about the future. The task of the poet is predicated on a prophetic power.

> In the last days of the fourth world I wished to make a
>   map for
> those who would climb through the hole in the sky.
>
> My only tools were the desires of humans as they emerged
>   from the killing fields, from the bedrooms and kitchens.
>
> For the soul is a wanderer with many hands and feet.[24]

That last line glistens with iconic power. But the voice is somber, making an incantatory music telling of the devastation that humans have visited on the earth.

To write poetry is to draw language "into the soft parts of my body" before it turns into hard bone. So out of word made flesh comes poetry, first flute breath of the trickster god.

Harjo often sings her poems in the manner of Native chants. She plays the saxophone with her band Poetic Justice. In New York City, in a packed auditorium I heard her play the saxophone and sing about a Nigerian man who drove a taxi in a harsh metropolis. Then she read a poem about a woman who walked through streets where lilacs blossomed, where space spun and curved and tapped her on the shoulder. Always in Harjo's work there's a fierce rhythm that seeks to etch itself through words

In a long note to the poem "Grace" she writes: "Rhythm starts from the inside, from the heart of the human, the planet, the solar system, the universe. It's coherence; it's the core."[25] As poet she touches the spirit that can soar through destruction, reach back for ancestral powers. A poetry that is penned at the rim of destruction draws on all the human faculties; a sixth sense leads the speaker on, through a world that she was not meant to survive.

I am reminded of what Gloria Anzaldúa, another visionary woman of the North American continent, has called "la facultad." In her *Borderlands / La Frontera,* Anzaldúa writes of this capacity "to see in surface phenomena the meaning of deeper realities . . . an instant sensing, a quick perception arrived at without conscious reasoning. It is an acute awareness by the part of the psyche that does not speak, that communicates in images and symbols." Anzaldúa continues on how this power "takes one from one's habitual grounding, causes the depths to open up, causes a shift in perception."[26] If for Anzaldúa this edgy, visionary power is linked to the *coatlicue* state, that uncanny condition where consciousness must face the uncertainty of all being, it is also for her the necessary condition for a new architecture.

In this too, it seems to me, Anzaldúa is close to Joy Harjo, for whom the house of poetry is something made up from the depths of what was destroyed. Consider this poem entitled "Returning from the Enemy":

> I peer out from the house I have constructed from the hole
>   in my heart,
> I have returned to the homelands beloved by my people
> who were marched to the west
> by the authority of a piece of paper[27]

Colonialism has dispossessed her people, rendered them exiles in their own land, and Harjo is a griot of this forced exile, one who sings the body and soul that must survive passage. If "vertigo," as she writes "is a terrible form of travel," it has led her to a precarious truth, the truth of passage.

In an early poem, "The Woman Hanging from the Thirteenth Floor Window," Harjo tells of a woman who is suspended between one life and the next, "a swirl of birds over her head." The whole of her existence flows through her consciousness. We see the sharp particulars that make up the glue of belonging, the wild rice she ate, the rocker she sat in, the two husbands who held her, the children she gave birth to. In between the long, incantatory stanzas a single line stands out: "She thinks she will be set free." The poem is deliberately, subtly crafted with two disparate endings, each of which evokes the psyche of this being who hangs, her life suspended in midair. Does she fall from the thirteenth floor or does she save herself? The reader must decide.

We realize that Harjo writes of people dispossessed, held in the grips of a cultural amnesia so acute that the poet has forgotten her own name in her native tongue. In "Returning from the Enemy" she writes:

> I have forgotten the reason, forgive me. *I have forgotten my name in the language I was born to, forgive me.*

The poem continues, the speaker rendered an internal exile in the country of her birth:

> I am trying to understand why the only story I can recall is drinking beer as a child on the beach of a man-made lake in Oklahoma. . . .
>
> I say nothing as a skiff of American tourists unloads at the dock with trailing, whining children.
>
> I say nothing because they appear to have inherited the earth.[28]

As Harjo recognizes, this is a postcolonial tale, a phrase she infuses with a fresh, mythic power in a poem of that title. "We emerge," the poet writes, "through dense unspeakable material."

Yet the earth is always beyond what words might reach. And

there is a humility in Harjo's lines, a sense of the sacred space that her predecessor on the North American continent, Walt Whitman, whose bardic ruminations were strung to the thread of a dominant ego, might well have longed for. In some ways Harjo is Whitman's spiritual daughter; for each the great power of the North American earth outpaces anything the poet might make. In a very short prose poem Harjo writes:

> This land is a poem of ochre and burnt sand I could never write, unless paper were the sacrament of sky, and ink the broken line of wild horses staggering the horizon several miles away. Even then, does anything written ever matter to the earth, wind and sky?[29]

Wild horses have written themselves against the sky. A mythic order beckons language. Is it a power that will draw the world out of violence into a new communion? The poet as mythmaker is also a warrior. "The poet in the role of a warrior is an ancient one," writes Harjo in a prefatory piece, her words evoking the spirit of Audre Lorde, one of Harjo's mentors, to whom she dedicated the early poem "Anchorage." In that poem the poet evokes a city "made of stone, of blood, of fish" where on a park bench an old grandmother lies bundled up. The ancestor who lies on a park bench, utterly dispossessed, becomes the necessary muse of a zone where words are edged with fire. At the end of that poem Harjo broods: "who would believe / the fantastic and terrible story of all of our survival, those who were never meant / to survive."[30]

The question of survival is etched deep into Yusef Komunyakaa's writing. Through his work I follow a fraught, interior journey and face a portion of the American story that would otherwise be hidden from me. He was born in 1947 into a black family in the segregated South, in Bogalusa, Louisiana, his father a carpenter, his maternal grandfather a penniless immigrant from the Caribbean who slipped onto American shores. In the poem "Mismatched Shoes" Komunyakaa evokes the unseen grandfather whose lost name he has taken as his own. The lines are short, sharp, filled with the syncopated breath of jazz, a mainstay for Komunyakaa, jazz the music of deprivation and hurt, of longing and desire, the ecstasy of the forbidden tongue:

> My grandfather came from Trinidad
> Smuggled in with a sack of papaya . . .
> He wore a boy's shoe
> and a girl's shoe with the taste
> of mango on his lips.
> Gone was his true name & deep song of Shango . . .[31]

Where will such ancestry lead him? In a 1998 interview he speaks about dreaming himself into other worlds, part of his growing up: "I would easily daydream about Mexico, Africa, or somewhere in Europe, and I later realized those daydreams were actually connected to where I was growing up—that there was a unique space, an eminent silence, from where I could project myself to other possibilities."[32]

"Eminent silence"—surely that is where the poems come from. While race for a poet like Adrienne Rich was something she had to come to learn, painfully, slowly, a reality that imploded during the heady years of the sixties, for Komunyakaa as a black child growing up in the South it is part and parcel of his awareness, intrinsic portion of the spiritual life that he lays claim to. Speaking of how jazz works into the poetry of black folk, he turns to figuration of language as bodily music. "I think I've said that lately I've been equating language as music and the body as an amplifier."[33] For him the idea of the body as amplifier for music is no mechanistic figuration; rather it is the flesh and blood of the body raced and sexed that stands at the heart of his vision. Elsewhere he recalls his Vietnam experience, a black man in an army fighting an indigenous people of color: "We cannot crawl out of our own skin, even when we try to lie to ourselves or say that race doesn't matter, that art and artists are color-blind, which is no more than an empty, delinquent illusion." The task for Komunyakaa even as he trawls wide and deep for his references—Catullus and Ovid, Baudelaire and Lorca—is to strip away the surfaces and stereotypes, to turn his racial origins into the very mirror of humanity. The gods, he muses in an essay, "work in severe darkness." Indeed, reading

Komunyakaa I am haunted by a darkness filled with music, a sounding on the pulse, the thrum and soar of the words.

But what of the specific task of poetry? It is 1984 and the poet is working on notes and poems about his Vietnam experience. He was a reporter on the field, saw combat, drew in the pain and racism of that war, understood through his skin and his bones what it was to endure danger. Back home he fixes up a house, fixes words, completing a set of Vietnam poems including "Starlight Scope Myopia." In that poem an apparatus of war is evoked; it "brings men into killing range." In the teeth of violence, the beauty of the scene makes the speaker breathless: "the river under Vi Bridge takes the heart away." He tries to lip-read what the enemy says, making "ghost talk." Are they laughing at the Americans, calling out in a mixture of tongues "*beaucoup dien cai dau*"? The phrase means crazy, very crazy, which is apparently what the Vietnamese called the Americans. The speaker sights an old man, part of the group of men lifting rice and ammunition. This is heavy work. A strange and fearful love seeps out:

> This one, old, bowlegged
>
> you feel you could reach out
> & take him into your arms. You
>
> peer down the sights of your M-16
> seeing the full moon
> loaded on an oxcart.[34]

Elsewhere he speaks of a kinship with the peasants, recalling his own ancestry, field workers in the American South. The lush landscape of his Louisiana childhood surfaces, a stippled memory that bonds him to paddy fields and trees and hills of Vietnam.

As he works on fixing up the house, he muses. "The ugly scars of history were all around me, and it became even more grotesque when moments of severe beauty showed through." His father and grandfather had been carpenters. The poet sets up his ladder, finds the necessary tools. He starts working in the intense heat. Down below, in another room, a deliberate distance away, he sets a pad of paper and a pen. He plays jazz, the hot syncopations that have entered his work. He starts to make what he calls "an imagistic narrative: a poem moved by the images and the inherent music in language."

The physical act of labor becomes a necessary pivot to his thought. Poetry is part of bodily being, desire inherent in the score of a line:

> Perched on the top rung of the ladder, each step down served as a kind of metrical device—made me plan each word and syllable. In the background, at the other end of the house, in the kitchen, jazz pulsed underneath the whole day. Sometimes I worked twelve to twenty hours. I realized that language is man's first music, and consequently, I began to approach the poem with this in mind.[35]

Language is music; language is also a choice of weapon with which to face a dangerous world. And this is a basic instinct that Komunyakaa shares with Harjo and Rich. For each poet, poetry must bear witness to what Adam Zagajewski has called "a mutilated world." The writing of poems becomes a ritual of cleansing, of making order. In "Facing It" Komunyakaa writes of his own face hidden in the black granite of the Vietnam memorial. As he traces the names, the stone seems to spill fire, a booby trap, the body forced into transparency, a vehicle for images that etch themselves into the torn consciousness. What Rich was to call the "segregate republic" is an intrinsic portion of this knowledge. At the very end the stone's black mirror holds a love that is inexplicable, luminous:

> A white vet's image floats
> closer to me, then his pale eyes
> look through mine. I'm a window.
> He's lost his right arm
> inside the stone. In the black mirror
> a woman is trying to erase names:
> No, she's brushing a boy's hair.[36]

The tenderness at the poem's end saves the speaker, saves the reader. In another poem, one of the most poignant of the war poems, "You and I are Disappearing," a girl cries inside the poet's head. She appears and disappears. The erotic is set aflame by incipient violence. Who is this girl who has entered the poet's skull and will not leave? What fierce fixation, what haunting? Is she the same woman who has turned into the muse who saves the poet's life in "Night Muse and Mortar Round," the female spirit who "shows up in every war"? Or is this the she of "Re-creating the Scene," a woman raped, then rising from the dust, her torn garments wrapped around her? The metamorphic power of the female body seals the wounds of the spirit. The one who is violated returns to haunt and to bless.

The autobiographical imperative impels the poet, driving his voice up through the tattered boards of history. Memory is worked into a deeply personal geography. There is an almost Keatsian ring to his words as he muses on *Magic City*, his 1992 volume published four years after the Vietnam volume: "So autobiography is also filled through with a number of hallways, like places on a map—sometimes there's a kind of clarity; rights and wrongs that make themselves known, other times there's a more blurred reality."[37]

The perception of this "blurred reality" allows Komunyakaa to lay bare the complex, striated truth of experience. "Tu Do Street" begins with the haunting line: "Music divides the evening." The poet broods on how "America pushes through the membrane / of mist and smoke." The black solider who cannot enter the brothel where the white soldiers throng pushes into the alleyways and finds a brothel where black GIs hold sway. Black and white touch through the sex of a Vietnamese woman, her flesh the conduit through which they taste each other's breath. The bodily economy is severe, part and parcel of purgatory.

A few years later, in the poems of childhood that cram every rift with sweetness, the voice turns to the early past as a way to invent a livable future, a mnemonic activity akin to self-preservation. The war zone was filled with ghosts, a place of emotional and physical flux. Now these poems of childhood map out a future, memory no stranger to joy. The five-year-old child in "Venus Fly Trap" wading out into sunlit grass knows bees can't live without flowers, and wonders why Daddy

Calls Mama honey.
All the bees in the world
Live in little white houses
Except the ones in these flowers
All sticky and sweet inside.
I wonder what death tastes like.
Sometimes I toss the butterflies
back into the air.[38]

In the brilliant, vertiginous "Nude Tango" a boy steals a choc-
olate rabbit from a refrigerator, enters the bedroom his parents
have left, and stands naked, swaying between two mirrors, his
shirt "a white flag." The themes of danger and violent surrender that the poet of *Dien Cai Dau* laid bare return in their
earliest incarnation, a child raped in a field, now in the safety
of his parents' bedroom, fronting the terror of memory, what
the body cannot bear, what the soul of the poet needs to remember in order to go on: "I tangoed one naked reflection /
Toward another creating a third." At the end of this meditation
where past and present layer into the requisite map, a grown
poet faces the child who must slip through mirrors, after violation able to kneel and dance. A harsh mercy is transmuted into
the veins of the poem:

I shoved out a hip
Threw my arms around
My image, & fell to the floor
To let it pass over
Like an animal traveling
Through our lives
To leave a mythic smell.[39]

What is this "mythic smell"? It is what the grandfather in his
mismatched shoes has led him to. What the woman who burns
on the hillside brings him, the night muse who faces the poet-
soldier. As always in Komunyakaa it is something that can only
be wrested through the interior journey, a beauty born of passage through violence. Now the revelation of a secret struggle
has all the poet's love, the pain worked to a knowledge that language must bear, "language . . . man's first music."

The roots of the world are held in the nest of the body. Natasha Trethewey understands this so clearly. The poems in her book *Native Guard* are fierce, tender evocations of a bodily existence touched by terror. The long title poem evokes the black soldiers who fought for the Union in the Civil War, their very existence under threat from their white comrades who had been known to fire on them. These long-lost voices are given to us through the fictive presence of a scribe among them: a freed slave, a letter-writer.

Then there are finely wrought, deeply personal poems about an "I." Her mother is black, her father white in a southern world where their marriage was a crime. For the speaker, race is precisely what makes her up and tears her apart. She bears witness to her life in intricate, elegant poems containing a voice that pierces to the quick of things, an unquiet zone where "the ghost of history lies down beside me." The speaker's mother has suffered a violent, abusive death. The voice bears witness to the maternal body laid to ground:

> her body—splintered
> clavicle, pierced temporal—her thin bones
> settling a bit each day, the way all things do.

History is a wound, almost unbearable, and beauty becomes the bright reversion, what permits us to bear witness, to endure, to turn again as we must to the necessary earth:

> I returned to a stand of pines,
>   bone-thin phalanx
>
> flanking the roadside, tangle
>   of understory. . . .
>
>   I return
>   to Mississippi, state that made a crime
>
> of me—mulatto, half-breed—native
>   in my native place, this place they'll bury me.[40]

Reading Trethewey's poems, we come face-to-face with traumatic memory and its hold on place. We are in the realm of

Toni Morrison's *Beloved*, fast-forwarded to a new generation. What Morrison's Sethe calls "rememory" sits squarely on the shoulders of Trethewey's speaker, allowing her to inhabit quite precisely what has been torn away. Such unsettlement is intrinsic to the imagination, awareness of ghostly inscriptions that exist out there in the shared realm, not isolated in a single mind, but as floating pictures in the world. In this roundabout way the dispossessed return to claim territory, stake out an impossible home:

> Places, places are still there. If a house burns down, its gone, but the place—the picture of it—stays, and not just in my rememory, but out there in the world. What I remember is a picture floating around, out there outside my head. I mean even if I don't think it, even if I die, the picture of what I did or knew, or saw, is still out there. Right in the place where it happened.

At the core of Sethe's beliefs is the sense of a bloodied world that persists. And in its wake comes memory, traumatic memory that can never be evaded, holding forth as it does in a perpetual present where nothing can alter the past. The places where the pain occurred exist for us, even as physical reality dies away. Traumatic memory, by bursting through the ordinary continuities of time, invests itself in a ceaseless present whose borders are mapped by sights and sounds that will never take leave of us precisely because we are forced to keep returning there, in our minds, over and over again. In this way, we come face-to-face with a symbolic landscape that even as it floats above time is vested in the truth of bodily being. Then too, it is a reality that has torn through the hold of a single consciousness and in its ghostliness, belongs to many others. The clear voice that Morrison has granted Sethe continues:

> Where I was before I came here, that place is real. It's never going away. Even if the whole farm—every tree and grass blade of it dies. The picture is still there and what's more, if you go there—you who never was there—if you go there and stand in the place where it was, it will happen again; it will be there for you, waiting for you.[41]

Such knowledge instills terror in the speaker. She forbids her daughter to ever return to that spot of ground, that unhallowed place. Places that exist as floating pictures make the past all too present. This, as Natasha Trethewey understands, is the paradox on which a wounded consciousness turns.

The poetry of Nathaniel Mackey shows us what happens when the hold of place is no longer necessary. In the epic poem *Splay Anthem* we leave the hold of place entirely and we enter a zone before things begin, and after they end—what Mackey calls "locality's discontent, ground gone under."

The title of the poem bears reflection. In the Oxford English Dictionary multiple definitions are given for the word *splay:*

1. To spread (the limbs, for example) out or apart, especially clumsily.
2. To make slanting or sloping; bevel.
3. To dislocate (a bone). Used of an animal.

The sloping ground of this poem results in a ceaseless mobility ("movement / the one mooring that we knew"). We face the restless, nervous motion of creatures perpetually dislocated. With loss of ground comes perpetual mobility, incandescent emotion and a fierce, stuttering music. Language is figured in its brokenness, fit for a stammering self and worthy of a migrant knowledge.

In his preface Mackey writes: "Lost ground, lost twinness, lost union and other losses variably inflect that aspiration, a wish among others, to be we, that of the recurring two, the archetypal lovers."

So it is that a sexual blossoming allows the poet to begin. Poetry has its source in desire:

> muse whose jutting
>   lips he kissed as he
> could . . . "Mouth that
>   moved my mouth,"
>   He
> soughed, hummed it,
>   made it buzz . . . Hummed,

hoped glass would break,
walls fall. Sang thru
                    the
         cracks a croaking
         song
   to end all song . . .

Desire draws us through exile, and its claim, the claim on lost
ground, keeps cropping up time and again. Lost ground, a no-
man's-land of traumatic memory, is where the poem is set, but
for Mackey there is a transcendent sense available here. Even as
beings who exist in no place etch out their lives through inces-
sant movement, the very agitation of their loss miraculously
bears fruit. The poem becomes a shelter, not for memory but
for what memory could not hold, the desire that impels one to
transgressive motion.

As readers, we witness a spectral existence, a ghostliness that
emerges, quite precisely because of the impossible nature of life
as given. So running makes its own zone where past, present,
and future all coexist, kingdom of perpetual exile:

   It was feeling's return we
   ran with, irredentist earth beneath
   our feet felt good. Irredentist earth
   fell away from our feet as we kept running.

And the constancy of running where there is no ground, allows
for a zone made up in the mind's space—desire's territory, a fictive thing:

   We made up ground
                    In a
   made-up landscape, no less real for that.
   Wind on us hard as it was we ran even faster.
                    Stride
   was our true country, native ground.[42]

While Trethewey's speaker hopes to be buried in a native
land that made a "crime of me," Mackey's selves race through
borderlands where it is impossible to come to a halt. No place

becomes a default home, and a entire poetics of dislocation springs up. We bear witness to the internal time of migrancy, and its painful, pleasurable flowering.

Gloria Anzaldúa has spoken of borderlands that come into being through radical loss. She figures this as a scab that bleeds, a shifting wound on the body politic: "It is in a constant state of transition. The prohibited and forbidden are its inhabitants."[43]

But in Mackey's poetry, the stuttering music that comes from the borderlands reveals an asymmetrically twinned couple, a *we*, precursor to any single subject, part and parcel of a raging mythos, a world before our current history of colonialism, slavery, and capitalism; a world where restless desire can make a dwelling place, where love might grant us an abode perfect in its persistence, a space of survival, shorn of the burden of fixity.

In Myung Mi Kim's work, fragments swirling in space maintain a fluid, if disrupted order. The poet was born in South Korea, and like Theresa Cha, Kim migrated to the United States. Nine years old when she arrived, she lived with her family in towns in Oklahoma, South Dakota, and Ohio. One wonders if this early mobility had implications for the poetry that emerged. Kim has staked out a difficult terrain brought into being through sharp, yet mobile particles of syntax. The story of exile and maternal longing that Cha embedded in *Dictée* has no place in Kim's work. Kim's antinarrative structures work their own elegant logic. In *Commons* the integument of things is torn away and we see bare, broken bones.

Places survive in ruins, and what remains stands in mute testimony to the violence wreaked by war. Kim's stanzas, often made up of words tugged from their accustomed moorings, reveal a persistent damage—damage to bodies and to inscriptions. And we catch glimpses of the power of memory to help us survive. It is in this zone of extremity that human beings struggle to build their lives. Dwelling happens in and through the detritus of civil society:

> Glyphs to alphabets. In which words have indications of time.
> They had to eat as much as they could in a hurry. Baskets
> woven by bloodlet fingers.

Minute fragments of what comes from our bodies as well as other natural bodies—skin, bone, stone, dirt, flower petals—become repositories of spiritual power, even as spectral voices tell of the dismemberment of living matter, the waste of flesh. In the sections of the poem entitled "Vocalise" we see how the activity of medical dissection opens up bodies for scrutiny, revealing the internal architecture of animal flesh.

In Kim's work, we stand in a state of perpetual aftermath. Bodies can no longer be presumed to be bound up with living breathing selves. But in this space of violent seizure, human beings survive, and voices start to utter through silence.

The structure of this long poem works in modes of accretion through numerical indices, through shining fractal parts that owe very little to the then–and then–and then requirements of story. There is no autobiographical "I" to be taken for granted, no necessary first-person subject. The serendipitous poet leads us away from the dense fixity of what we thought matter to be. And somehow through it all, a lyric beauty persists, and natural rhythms of light, and falling water or snow:

> Terms stringent for lack of food
> Root insect berry pass a mud inscription
> Place where
>
> Weeks of slaughter and remonstrance
> Fed the children and animals first
> Without interruption the entry log of days
>
> Snow may be falling.[44]

Survival becomes a métier, earnestly desired. We catch the workings of a poet in a space of affliction, rendered crystalline through the power of imagination.

4.

In our beginning is our end. The imagination makes room for the poem, and the poem in turn makes place substantial to the imagination. Indeed it is the task of the poem to create place.

The new American poet understands that this applies also to the borderlands that make up her true home.

She returns in the evening to the apartment where she has lived for many years, at the northern end of an island city. The building stands on a boulder of granite, an outcrop of an older topography. She thinks she will sit and write a few lines for a poem. But as she stoops to pick up her notebook she glimpses the book with the blue covers with the picture of clouds in the open sky. The name of the poet is just beneath the image. He is a great poet of exile, who died an untimely death, not so long ago. His death in this very country saddens her. She has never met him but she has heard his poems read out, in a rich, sorrowful voice, in a city at the edge of the Blue Nile where she lived as a teenager.

She picks up the book and opens it at random. Her eyes light on lines at the top of the page and she flips back to find the start of the sentence. The passage has to do with the death of friends in a time of war, with the loss of place, station, name:

> It's as if we were here as caretakers of fragile substances and were now preparing to absorb the operation of moving our reality, in its entirety, into the domain of memories forming within sight of us. . . . We'll part in the pitch of longing.[45]

She understands that this is the task of the poet, to be a caretaker of "fragile substances"—sensuous perceptions, embodied memories, desire that strikes out into a future that would otherwise never exist.

She senses that in the complex, interlocking gestures of new American poetry, a powerful capillary action is at work. The world in all its multiplicity is absorbed within, cast into a shimmering network of sense.

She feels this is how the terror of history is assuaged, how time is made habitable.

She sets the book with the blue covers down gently, next to a thick tattered volume. Its pages that have come unstuck from the binding are heavily marked. She feels another self must have marked out those lines, but they resonate for her, as if she knew them already, and she feels as if she were swimming in a mnemonic paradise. Words fill with echoes, lines clarify as she reads:

> See, steamers steaming through my poems
> See, in my poems immigrants continually coming and
> landing . . .
> See, on the one side the Western Sea and on the other the
> Eastern Sea, how they advance and retreat upon my own
> poems as upon their own shores . . .[46]

The poem becomes a place where the world is born again. The difference between that older time and this, she realizes, is that now those migrant memories, only hinted at earlier, are sufficiently copious to make up their own discrepant history, a history that is coequal with the chaos of belonging, with the melancholy truth of departure and the exhilaration of arrival.

She stares into the mirror. In the half darkness her own face appears, dark, edged with sudden sunlight. She lifts up her hands to the mirror, the hands with which she must write the poem that is in her, but they have turned into two shadows, butterflies that threaten to fly away.

NOTES

1. Mahmoud Darwish, *Memory for Forgetfulness,* trans. Ibrahim Muhawi (Berkeley and Los Angeles: University of California Press, 1995), 11.

2. Édouard Glissant, *Poetics of Relation,* trans. Besty Wing (Ann Arbor: University of Michigan Press, 2000), 29, 30, 40.

3. Zygmunt Bauman, *Identity: Conversations with Benedetto Vecchi* (Malden, MA: Polity Press, 2004), 20.

4. Frances Yates, *The Art of Memory* (Chicago: University of Chicago Press, 1974), 2.

5. Gilles Deleuze and Félix Guattari, *A Thousand Plateaus: Capitalism and Schizophrenia,* trans. Brian Massumi (Minneapolis: University of Minnesota Press, 1987), 11.

6. Seamus Heaney, "The Place of Writing," in *Finders Keepers: Selected Prose, 1971–2001* (New York: Farrar, Straus and Giroux, 2002), 253, 255.

7. Agha Shahid Ali, "Evanescence," in *A Nostalgist's Map of America* (New York: Norton, 1991), 41–42, 58.

8. Agha Shahid Ali, *Rooms Are Never Finished* (New York: Norton, 2002),100.

9. A. K. Ramanujan, *Collected Poems* (New Delhi: Oxford University Press, 1995), 7, 126, 151, 122–23.

10. A. K. Ramanujan, *Collected Essays* (New Delhi: Oxford University Press, 1999), 35–36.

11. A. K. Ramanujan, *The Interior Landscape* (New Delhi: Oxford University Press, 1967), 19.

12. Derek Walcott, *Collected Poems, 1948–1984* (New York: Farrar, Straus and Giroux, 1986), 346.

13. Derek Walcott, *What the Twilight Says* (New York: Farrar, Straus and Giroux, 1998).

14. Walter Benjamin, *Illuminations*, ed. Hannah Arendt, trans. Harry Zohn (New York: Schocken, 1969), 78, 79.

15. Walcott, *Collected Poems*, 161, 197–99, 145, 208–9.

16. Derek Walcott, "Muse of History," in *What the Twilight Says*, 40.

17. Jean Arasanayagam, *Reddened Water Flows Clear* (London: Forest Books, 1991), 116.

18. Quoted by Minoli Salgado, *Writing Sri Lanka: Literature, Resistance, and the Politics of Place* (London: Routledge, 2007), 75.

19. Arasanayagam, *Reddened Water Flows Clear,* 86, 62.

20. Anna Deveare Smith, *Fires in the Mirror* (New York: Anchor, 1993), xxxiv.

21. Smith, *Fires in the Mirror,* xxiv, 12.

22. Theresa Cha, *Dictee* (Berkeley: Third Woman Press, 1995), 73.

23. Joy Harjo, *How We Became Human: New and Selected Poems* (New York: Norton, 2002), 131.

24. Harjo, *How We Became Human,* 129.

25. Harjo, *How We Became Human,* 129, 154, 215.

26. Gloria Anzaldúa, *Borderlands / La Frontera: The New Mestiza* (San Francisco: Aunt Lute Books, 1987), 60–61.

27. Harjo, *How We Became Human,* 152–53.

28. Harjo, *How We Became Human,* 154, 162, 163.

29. Harjo, *How We Became Human,* 58.

30. Harjo, *How We Became Human,* 152–53, 154, 162–63, 58, xxvii, 32.

31. Yusef Komunyakaa, *Pleasure Dome: New and Collected Poems* (Middletown, CT: Wesleyan University Press, 2001), 292.

32. Yusef Komunyakaa, *Blue Notes: Essays, Interviews, and Commentaries* (Ann Arbor: University of Michigan Press, 2000), 99.

33. Komunyakaa, *Blue Notes,* 92.
34. Komunyakaa, *Pleasure Dome,* 195.
35. Komunyakaa, *Blue Notes,* 15.
36. Komunyakaa, *Pleasure Dome,* 235.
37. Komunyakaa, *Blue Notes,* 87.
38. Komunyakaa, *Pleasure Dome,* 258.
39. Komunyaka, *Pleasure Dome,* 287.
40. Natasha Trethewey, *Native Guard* (Boston: Houghton Mifflin, 2006), 11, 46.
41. Toni Morrison, *Beloved* (New York: Plume, 1988), 35, 36.
42. Nathaniel Mackey, *Splay Anthem* (New York: New Directions, 2002), x, 70, xi, 3, 86, 100.
43. Anzaldúa, *Borderlands / La Frontera,* 3.
44. Myung Mi Kim, *Commons* (Berkeley and Los Angeles: University of California Press, 2002), 6, 23.
45. Mahmoud Darwish, *Memory for Forgetfulness,* 59–60.
46. Walt Whitman, "Starting from Paumanock," in *Leaves of Grass,* ed. Sculley Bradley and Harold W. Blodgett (New York: Norton, 1973), 27.

Night Music

The poetry of Adrienne Rich makes a night music. I sit in my mother's house in Kerala in the half darkness of a monsoon night, a single bulb burning to my right, the sounds of night creatures in the courtyard filling my ears. Lines of her poetry sound in my head. Her words float out of the mango trees and there is no dissonance here, I carry my interior world with me.

In my other life, I live in an apartment near the river Hudson, and as the bird flies, not far from Paterson, New Jersey, where William Carlos Williams lived for many years. He was a doctor. He treated the sick. He birthed babies. When I first arrived in America, I made a pilgrimage to Paterson, a place I had only heard of through poems. I saw splintered streets, colorful cafes, shop windows boarded up, a factory by water that fell in white threads, spilling over the stone lip of the cliff.

Later I read his lines again. They lie at the heart of a great love poem "Of Asphodel that Greeny Flower." Years later I used their resonance in a poem I wrote, set in the New York City subways, which I called "News of the World": a poem about immigrants.

Those lines by Williams serve to preface Adrienne Rich's 1993 *Notebooks on Poetry and Politics,* no accident I think, for Rich is one of the most overtly political of contemporary American poets, one who reflects time and again on the transfiguring power of the poem and how it allows us to dwell in community.

Here are the lines from William Carlos Williams that haunt me:

> It is difficult
> to get the news from poems
>   yet men die miserably every day for lack
> of what is found there.

What is found there?

A question that might well have no clear discernable answer, forcing one to sink into the elemental, the unspeakable.

In an essay called "The Distance between Language and Violence," Rich speaks in the third person of the child that she was, trying through the force of mnemonic figuration to spell out the power that drove her to write: "Early on, she experiences language, especially poetry, as power: an elemental force that is *with* her, like the wind at her back as she runs across a field."[1]

In this essay Rich dwells on the taken-for-granted racism of the white world in which she found herself. The education she received made believe the question of race did not exist, a forced dissociation of sense that took her decades to overcome. She tells of a memory that will not leave her: how as a young child she flung a tin shovel at the black woman who was taking care of her, how the metal cut the woman's forehead and the child was made to say sorry. The shame of it does not leave the poet. What became of the black woman? We do not know.

In her poem "Power" about Marie Curie, Rich writes: "She died a famous woman denying / her wounds / denying her wounds came from the same source as her power."

In her poem, "The Fact of a Doorframe," we glimpse the connections she forges between language, violence and poetic self-fashioning:

> I think of the story of the goose-girl who passed through the
>   high gate
> where the head of her favorite mare
> was nailed to the arch
> and in a human voice
> If she could see thee now, thy mother's heart would break
> said the head of Falada
>
> Now, again, poetry
> violent, arcane, common,
> hewn of the commonest living substance
> into archway, portal, frame
> I grasp for you, your bloodstained splinters, your
> ancient and stubborn poise
> —as the earth trembles—
> burning out from the grain[2]

In the epic sequence "Atlas of a Difficult World," published seven years later in 1991, the task of poetry fuses with the physical labor needed to sustain the human world, a world torn apart in a "segregate republic."

I am put in mind of Oothoon's prophetic cry in *Visions of the Daughters of Albion*. And indeed William Blake, the great poet of English romanticism deeply misunderstood in his own lifetime, is one of her influences. Rich has written of how as a child she would copy Blake's lines into her notebook. Again speaking of her childhood self in the third person, Rich tells us how the child who has copied in lines from "Tyger, tyger burning bright" receives grades in her notebook only for the quality of her handwriting. The book *Atlas of a Difficult World* taps into Blake's prophetic voice, the Blake who in his "Visions of the Daughters of Albion" made Oothoon cry out a fierce indictment of a fallen world, a world of gins and traps, joys bent out of shape, and the pleasure of the body distorted by repressive power. A buried river leads from Blake's Oothoon to Rich's speaker who punctuates space on the page, marking the pauses breath needs for meaning to clarify:

> Waste. Waste. The watcher's eye put out, hands of the
>   builder severed, brain of the maker starved
> those who could bind, join, reweave, cohere, replenish
> now at risk in this segregate republic[3]

The dream of a common language still binds the poet, a language that moves through violation into an imagined space of healing. And language, as she says elsewhere, is always tied to "music, the vibration of a voice."[4] So the voice of this poet, precise, pained, celebratory, must raise into the light "the gaunt original thing / gristle and membrane of your life" ("Two Arts," *Atlas*, 54). If such autobiographical musing can be a "brutal thing," this is precisely because history is inextricably woven in with the truth of the body. For Rich, the art of poetry has no other locus.

In the 1983 poem "North American Time"—we know the date of composition because it is given at the end of each of her poems, a marker anchoring the poem in the continuum of a life lived—Rich reveals how words might be used against the intentions of the one who crafted them, how words live and breathe and flutter and burn quite apart from the hands of the maker. And this is what the freedom of the artist amounts to: "Poetry never stood a chance / of standing outside history." "North American time" summons her and there is no escape. Underlying the compulsion to words, the drive to write that binds a poet with hurt arthritic hands to her typewriter, is a visionary power, the necessity to bear witness.

The Julia de Burgos she speaks of in the concluding stanza of the poem is a Puerto Rican poet and revolutionary who died in abject poverty on the streets of New York. The island city becomes in these stanzas the bedrock for reflection where meaning must be made. Here history is layered over itself, cast into a palimpsest of memory. Here African graves and Native burial mounds are torn and pilfered, sealed over with modern buildings made of brick and concrete. Here the poet climbing up the battered stairs, sits at her typewriter, discovers her voice:

> The almost-full moon rises
> timelessly speaking of change
> out of the Bronx, the Harlem river
> the drowned towns of the Quabbin
> the pilfered burial mounds
> the toxic swamps, the testing-grounds
> and I start to speak again[5]

The pain of history teaches the poet how to praise. There is a plainness to the voice, a straightforward laying of thing as they are, necessary anchorage for the fiery prophetic timbres when they come. In the house of my grandparents, ghosts now, I hear her voice. It moves the dark, so the outlines of things as they are, clarify. The poet's voice is borne in the night wind, a promise of life, of survival.

NOTES

1. Adrienne Rich, *What Is Found There: Notebooks on Poetry and Politics* (New York: Norton), 183.

2. Adrienne Rich, *The Fact of a Doorframe* (New York: Norton, 1981), prefatory page.

3. Adrienne Rich, *Atlas of the Difficult World* (New York: Norton, 1991), 11.

4. *Adrienne Rich's Poetry and Prose* (New York: Norton, 1975), 258.

5. *Adrienne Rich's Poetry and Prose*, 118.

45

Encountering Emily

There are poets rooted in the American soil, whose work I had read long before I came to the United States. My mind turns to Emily Dickinson and Walt Whitman, poets who belong to the world at large.

Encountering Emily. How did it happen for me? Her lines leap and I duck, turn skittish. Her voice does not leave my head. I am scared and it has taken me decades to return to that radiant vision. I came upon her poems when I was twelve or thirteen, and living for part of each year in a hot country, just south of the Sahara desert. It was Khartoum, in summer time, 114 degrees in the shade. In the school library I came upon a battered book, an anthology, the covers were peeling.

What was it, that book, I ask myself in an attempt to be precise. I cannot tell, though I can still recall the size and shape and the covers, worn beyond legibility. It was there I found a few of her poems. "Wild nights" was there, how can I forget it? I took the book home, logging in my name in my best handwriting in the library ledger.

I sat on the gravel at the edge of the verandah, in the shade of a neem tree. I could see the dark dates on the date palm on the manicured lawn, the blinding blue of a sky without rain, just south of the Sahara desert. Her words cut straight to the heart of what I felt to be my secret life, all that my mother and the centuries of a strict patriarchal tradition had crossed out, desire with nowhere to inscribe itself, fled to the dark waters of secrecy:

#269

Wild nights—Wild nights!
Were I with thee
Wild nights should be
Our luxury!

Futile—the winds—
To a Heart in port—
Done with compass—
Done with the chart!

Rowing in Eden—
Ah—the Sea!
Might I but moor—tonight—
In thee!¹

"Futile—the Winds." I loved the pause there, after the word "futile" and I murmured the words to myself, they entered my inner ear. I learned that poem by heart. I was used to learning poems by heart, Wordsworth, Verlaine, Shelley, Rimbaud, all manner of lyrics that my strict colonial education led me to, in the girl's school that housed my early years. Emily Dickinson's poems seemed so well suited for "by hearting," as it was called. In India some portion of a good upbringing involved learning to memorize the classics, bits of Tagore and Vallathol, Mirabai and the Psalms from the Bible.

Though Dickinson as an American poet had played no part in the classical world that was laid out for me as an inheritance, and perhaps even in part because of this lack, I clung to her. She was my secret. I glimpsed the life of a grown girl forced to turn inwards, in a poise so fierce that it fled what commonly passed for decorum. And through her I touched a lyricism that imploded the bounding lines of grammar.

I say this for in those early years when I wanted so very much to be a poet, and nothing but, the peculiar fixity of English as I encountered it seemed to be designed quite precisely to keep me from myself. This was where my friendship with Emily came in.

In my dreams, much as a swimmer might, I dove under the dividing lines of languages, Malayalam my mother tongue, Hindi, English, French, Arabic and then I swam very fast. And Emily was my secret swimming companion.

Now there was no way I could possibly have formulated what passed through my head in the way I have put it down here. Far from it, but these were thoughts, if I might call them that, or even sensations, so true, I had no words for them. In those days, my great concerns acknowledged by my conscious self were how to escape my mother's slow designs to lead me into life through the portals of an arranged marriage, and my father's designs to teach me the truths of Newtonian physics. Poetry seemed to me to be the way to cull the blossoms of an interior life, one which was answerable to no one. So I turned to Emily, whose lines once encountered were hard to evade. It seemed to me that she had understood something that no one else had.

#710

> Doom is the House without the Door
> 'Tis entered from the Sun—
> And then the Ladder's thrown away,
> Because Escape—is done—

The first line of this poem kept returning to me in dreams, with the dull thud thud of the "d" sound, ontology of an impossible life, end to everything.

No wonder then, and I realize it now, though earlier I had clean forgotten, after the line "Because Escape—is done—" comes a stanza that leads us away from the house without a door, to a dream of what happens outside. This is a realm as exterior as things can get in Dickinson—"Where Squirrels play—and Berries dye—" a space where phenomena paint themselves over a realm of fatal necessity, essential ephemera, maya.

And I use the word *maya,* familiar to me from childhood, from the strict Advaitic philosophy my maternal grandfather schooled me in, Sankara's word for the realm of all passing phenomena, field of the sensorium.

Perhaps this is why I could not remember that stanza at all, written by a poet perpetually haunted by elsewhere, though Puritan necessity fed her, nourished her febrile lines. I will spell out the second stanza so that the whole of this poem appears:

> 'Tis varied by the Dream
> Of what they do outside—
> Where squirrels play—and Berries dye—
> And Hemlocks—bow to God—

And now as I read them again, those lines put me in mind of another great woman poet, Akkamahadevi, also known as Mahadevyakka, from the classical bhakti tradition of India, writing in Kannada, the sharp aphoristic words she composed in the twelfth century CE, animated by desire so impossible that it burned up flesh, illicit love of Lord Siva to whom she proclaimed herself betrothed as she wandered about, her sari torn off, clad only in her long flowing black hair.

Here is one of Akkamahadevi's poems, a Kannada vacana in A. K. Ramanujan's inimitable translation:

> Like a silkworm weaving
> her house with love
> from her marrow,
>   and dying
> in her body's threads
> winding, tight, round
> and round,
>   I burn
> desiring what the heart desires.
>
> Cut through, O lord,
> my heart's greed,
> and show me
> your way out,
> O lord white as jasmine.[2]

To return to Emily, clearly she did not wander around naked. Her white gowns, her bonnets, her life within the compound and streets of Amherst are justly celebrated. Yet in her poetry she did roam, far, wide, stripping herself free, at times with great difficulty, of all that might trammel her. And so it is in Emily Dickinson, rather than in Akkamahadevi, the latter surely closer to home in terms of the traditions I was born to, that I have found an iconic instance of what I think of as a poetics of dislocation.

I am speaking of the way in which for Emily Dickinson, the joints of what one commonly takes for granted, the everyday, have come apart and into the multiple gashes rendered so cryptically in her lines, a species of eternity enters in.

If for Akkamahadevi desire spins out the cocoon of death, for

Dickinson death is the silk of impossible desire, a fabric that sears, terrible predicate of love. How else to make sense of the quivering identity at the heart of her enterprise, that blinding lyric flash possessed by no other poet I can think of.

#647

> To fill a Gap
> Insert the thing that caused it—
> Block it up
> With other—and twill yawn the more—
> You cannot solder an Abyss
> with Air.

All that is solid peels away and the soul is left haunted by an unerring sense of what she elsewhere names "bright Absentee," first cousin surely to Mallarmé's "L'absente de tous bouquets."

To round off, I turn to a few lines composed by Emily Dickinson in 1862, just a year after "Wild Nights," a poem in which the present exists as a figment, a slash of light without which one could not live, and underpinning it, a spiritual longing touched by despair, revealing an art of extremity as sharp and clear as anything the mortal mind is capable of conceiving. As I read the poem again I think of how these lines have an eerie connection to our lives at the edge of the twenty-first century. They seem to me utterly contemporary.

There is a journey, she calls it "our journey," and almost at a fork in the road where eternity starts, the speaker halts. Before the cities which one imagines filled with people, comes the "Forest of the Dead." No explanation is given, for this strange and yet seemingly natural turn of topology in a time of war.

#453

> Retreat—was out of Hope—
> Behind—a Sealed Route—
> Eternity's White Flag—Before—
> And God—at every Gate

In a mystical transformation, wounds have turned into gates, sites of perpetual surrender, portals to divinity.

Published in *TriQuarterly* 122 (2005)

An earlier version was presented at the Emily Dickinson celebration with Marie Ponsot and Karen Malpede, American Studies Group, CUNY Graduate Center, March 31, 2004. My thanks to Audrey Raden, who invited me to speak.

1. All quotations of Dickinson are from *The Poems of Emily Dickinson*, ed. R. W. Franklin (Cambridge: Harvard University Press, 1999).

2. A. K. Ramanujan, *Speaking of Śiva* (Harmondsworth: Penguin, 1973), 116.

In Whitman's Country

I too had receiv'd identity by my body,
That I was I knew was of my body, and what I should be I knew
I should be of my body.
—Walt Whitman, "Crossing Brooklyn Ferry"

How could I have come to the United States without Whitman? Sometimes in times of difficulty, when reinvention of the self is a fierce necessity—a time such as now—I think of myself as having been wafted here by Walt, a creature with a tumbling gray beard, cap askew, bony wings sprouting out of his corduroy jacket.

There are bits of grass in his mouth and when I am about to pass out, with all the air gushing through—we make a curious kind of airplane together—he pushes a few stalks into my mouth. The grass is filled with moisture, rather cold and glittery and the bits of ice on the blades help moisten my tongue. I totter a little with the unsteadiness of it all. Am I on a "trottoir," as he called it? Am I really in Manhattan?

I could not have come to America without Whitman. Now that would be an odd statement to make to an officer at the other end of the table when one is taking a citizenship test—How many Stars, how many Stripes, how many States? etc. What should I say? Whitman drew me here, and now I am a woman who must cast herself on the kindness of others:

> I resist anything better than my own diversity,
> Breathe the air but leave plenty after me,
> And am not stuck up, and am in my place.
> ("Song of Myself" #16)[1]

November 2, 2004. It's a moist fall day and I put on a light coat and go to take my place in the line at the polling booth near Fort Tryon Park. I was born in India, the world's most populous democracy and it is in India, where I returned after my studies in England, that I read Whitman again, with great intensity. In me are the memories of voting lines in Hyderabad where I used to live before I came here, old people who had trudged in from villages miles away, mothers with infants hoisted to their hips, laborers, teachers, and everywhere the dust rising in the dryness that gripped the city before the rains fell. Now in the dampness of November I step into the sunlight and my fingers close around the pages I have slipped into my pocket. The pages are dry and light and they feel as if a current of air were still passing through them.

When I first came here, I bought a book. I see from the date on the front page, December 1979, that I had purchased it a little over a month after I arrived in Manhattan. Books were a luxury then, but this was one I did not want to be without—Whitman's *Leaves of Grass*. Even now, the pencil markings I made so long ago are vivid, new to me, just as the book is, though the glue is resolutely unstuck in that green-backed Norton edition and I can tear out hunks and carry pages with me without hurting the boundaries of poems. So it is that "Song of Myself" torn loose of the book has come to take up residence in my coat pocket. And I have recourse to the poem as I stand waiting for the old man in glasses to check out my signature, neatly xeroxed in the pad of voters' names in front of him. I am all ready for a hitch, but it seems to work, the tally of name and signature as I point out my address, the very last apartment building on Fort Washington Avenue, just before the park. How far north can one go on this island and not fall into water? Just a few more miles towards Spuyten Duyvil and one can see the gray rocks lapping at the foam.

Every few years I go through a blaze of reading Whitman and there are always poems I return to, in some driven way: "Song of Myself," "Crossing Brooklyn Ferry," and from time to time "Out of the Cradle." So it was before I left India in late 1979, so it is now. Why?

It has to do with identity. Identity, that overused, much maligned word. In a recent book of that title Zygmunt Bauman speaks of the "specter of exclusion" that haunts us in this age of fluid, coursing borders.[2] And it is precisely to that anxious reality that Whitman speaks. Reading the poet when I was a young woman in India, I was gripped by an excitement that is still in me when I open his pages.

Who else has conceived of the self as a cluster of jutting, jostling identities and dared to make an epic out of that chaos, cutting and clipping it into a *paysage état d'âme* that is pronounced to be coextensive with a great continent? Who else has made such music out of self-division and then imagined a new, internally embattled nation as coequal to that self?

I purchased my now battered copy of *Leaves of Grass* and went walking over Brooklyn Bridge. It was one of the first things I wanted to do in Manhattan, see that bridge and if possible walk over it. It was a clear cold day. I had not felt such cold since leaving England six years earlier. The air was brilliant and clear. I felt a sense of elation at the sweet metallic grid that upheld the bridge and staring down at the waters below murmured the lines as if they were a blessing:

> Saw the reflection of the summer sky in the water,
> Had my eyes dazzled by the shimmering track of beams,
> Look'd at the fine centrifugal spokes of light round the
> shape of my head in the sunlit water . . .
>
> ("Crossing Brooklyn Ferry" #3)

As a child in a mixture of awe and terror I had stared down at my own forbidden reflection in the well. The waters were dark, and sixty feet down was a blurred image of a girl. Everything was misty as I stared down into the water I was told might swallow me if I looked. But I looked anyway. And what the darkness of well water gave back, still haunts me. Here, though was the possibility of brilliant sunshine, a benediction around a face, a blessing for a body that dared to cross a bridge.

I remember looking up and seeing across the water the grim sign of Jehovah's Witnesses, a Watchtower sign, something I was familiar with from India. The end of the world, it was everywhere, in everything and Whitman had dared to flow through into a eternal present that for me seemed vouchsafed in the idea of America.

Where else could I have come to from a country where the weight of centuries threatened to overwhelm? It seemed to me there was an odd fit between the burden of time I was born to and the promise of space that I had chosen. But what sort of life could I make for myself here, what sort of poetry? Those were questions that only time would slowly answer.

Yet Whitman did not abandon me. Just last year, in March 2003 when I was working a poem I eventually called "Triptych in a Time of War" I felt that pulse of anxiety which sometimes hits me when writing, the sense that I was entering utterly uncharted territory.[3] I was writing in a time of war. It was then I felt the presence of Whitman, the feeling that it was all right, to go ahead and write in the strum and throb of a violent present, make a long line for the breath to weave through, try and make sense of multiple worlds, one layering over the other, make an American poem, whatever in God's name that might be.

And what of 'The old knot of contrariety' that we see evoked in "Crossing Brooklyn Ferry" and throughout Whitman's poetry, the tug of opposing elements, the dark, the hidden, the silenced, braided through the clear and sweet and light. There was a way in which Whitman spoke utterly directly to the knotted, secretive life I had led. I was raised in a world of tradition and decorum where being born a girl meant that even if one were to receive an education, and excel in that realm of thought and learning, the sexual self was already mortgaged, bound into a shadowy space of indebtedness. Hence the self-division that I learned to live with, depending on the mind to free me, if only provisionally. For after all, who could lose her body? I will never forget the frisson that ran down my spine when I read the line: "Through me many long dumb voices" ("Song of Myself" #24).

Mine was a world in which one could be ritually cast out. A world in which one could be born outcaste, was never far from me, in spite of the many miles I traveled as a child, from continent to continent, crossing waters far from Kerala. I think of Lalithambika Antherjanam, the great Malayalam writer born ninety years after Whitman, and two continents away, on the

55

southwest coast of India, in what is now Kerala. I think of the continental plates rubbing together as if the mists of time were upon us. The poet from "fish-shape Paumanok" whispers to the poet born from a bolt of land said to have risen from an ax Parasurama tossed into the Arabian Sea. For Lalithambika started as a poet though she went on to write in prose. Whitman draws his beard aside and whispers to her:

> This is the meal equally set, this the meat for natural
>   hunger,
> It is for the wicked just the same as the righteous, I make
>   appointments with all,
> I will not have a single person slighted or left away,
> The kept-woman, sponger, thief, are hereby invited,
> The heavy-lipp'd slave is invited, the venerealee is invited;
> There shall be no difference between them and the rest.

("Song of Myself" #19)

The ritual displacement of women in traditional Namboodiri society forms the core of Lalithambika's work and stands at the heart of her novel *Agnisakshi* (*Trial by Fire*). The self doubles, splits into two: the self that endures, mute, voiceless, and the other self that bears witness, taking on the role of narrator. In the struggle with the prescriptions of an all-powerful culture, her own bodily self, passionate, desiring, violated, silenced, becomes the very source of speech. Elsewhere in my writing I have called this a "back against the wall aesthetic," a recourse to the most primitive ground: the body as the site of first and last resort.[4] And it is precisely here I see her rubbing shoulders with Walt Whitman. In her sleep she speaks to him, and he a gay man shares with her the evidence of the senses, a vision of "the caresser of life wherever moving" ("Song" #13).

I have no evidence that Lalithambika read Whitman. In fact it's very possible that she didn't. But Whitman certainly has been translated into my mother tongue Malayalam, an ancient coastal language of India, whose literature has been fed as all great literatures have been, by the streams of translation. Kerala has a long socialist tradition and Pushkin and Tolstoy, Neruda and Lorca and Whitman have all been translated into Malayalam. When I was a child in Kerala I used to hear cousins who went to school reciting bits of Whitman that they had "by hearted" in Malayalam, part of a long mnemonic tradition.

In a recent email communication I asked the poet Ayyappa Paniker about Whitman. He had sent me, in English translation, his poem entitled "Yesterday, I Saw Whitman." The poem has a poignant opening:

Yesterday, or was it the day before, I saw Whitman.
Talking loudly about the multitudes,
In loneliness I saw Whitman.
Stretching his long shadow across the Long Island,
the islander poet was counting the waves of the sea.[5]

The email he sent with the poem was eloquent. Ayyappa Paniker, one of the great twentieth-century poets of Malayalam, told me that he connected Whitman in his imagination with another epic poet, Vyasa, the author of the *Mahabharata*. Both were born on islands. Then turning to the other great Indian epic, news of which might well have reached Whitman's ears, Ayyappa Paniker writes, "The remaining or solitary bird in 'Out of the Cradle' perhaps echoes the survivor bird in the story of Valmiki, the author of the *Ramayana*." He ends by speaking of the "invisible threads" that surely bind us, telling me of an old man who lived in the city of Thirvananthapuram who so loved Emerson, that everyone knew him by that name—Emerson. He concludes his email by saying: "In the metreless metre of recent Malayalam poetry we may see the influence of Whitman, Neruda, Lorca etc."[6]

As a small child in Kerala I used a stick to draw pictures in the dirt. Often I would draw rooms and even houses and then try to join them together in a figure of eight. Then I would use my bare feet to make the drawings disappear and all that was left was the rippling figure of eight, that too disappearing in the garden dirt.

This summer I was in Kerala to visit my mother who lives the house of her childhood and mine. It is built in the traditional *nalukettu* manner, red tiles and whitewashed walls, enclosing a gravel-covered courtyard where a mulberry bush still grows. She wanted to consult a lawyer about making a will and we traveled to the ancient port city of Kochi to find a lawyer. The waters of the Arabian sea were deep blue, a seamless silk drawn up and shook out into tiny gleaming waves. In Mattancherri Palace I stopped short, breathless, in front of a wall full of old maps of Kochi.[7] These maps seemed bland, colorless next to the room of intricate murals I had just passed through, the far wall filled to bursting with scenes of childbirth in the *Ramayana,* a unique set of images, the almond-eyed royal infants dropping clean out of their mothers' thighs, three boy babies in brilliant vegetable colors, seventeenth-century imaginings of grace and courtliness, a dream of bodily continuity.

And the maps? The maps were Dutch, from the same period, representations of Kochi harbor. What made me stand still was their eerie semblance to maps of New Amsterdam, made in the same period, the stylized mainland, the curved passageways for water, Vypeen Island, Governor's Island, they blurred and doubled in my mind's eye. The Dutch had lost New Amsterdam to the British in 1664, precisely a year after they took Kochi from the British. This figure of eight stays with me—gaining Cochin and access to the spice trade in 1663; losing New Amsterdam. It takes a mythic turn in my mind and I imagine the waters of the Indian Ocean and the Atlantic, which I have criss-crossed in my life.

I need to stay with this loop in time and space, this fluid figure of motion and see how far it will take me. I need to pay attention to where the figure ruptures and how I might set down a small shelter made of words, a poem. And saying all this, it is clear to me, that without Whitman I could never have come this far.

Tomorrow morning if the weather is fine I will put on my boots and walk north to the edge of the island, to Spuyten Duyvil. The northern side of the creek was called Shorakapok by the Lenape people who inhabited it. The word is translated as "space between the ridges" or "sitting down place." I will sit between the rocks and gaze at the waters of the river Hudson. My grandmother was born in Kozhikode, an ancient city where Vasco da Gama landed. I imagine Whitman, his beard speckled with salt spray, strolling where the Arabian sea meets the land of Kerala.

Now I sit here at the Hudson's edge, haunted by what the poet in "Out of the Cradle" called "the unknown want." I search for something that lies just beyond the reach of words, in Whitman's country.

NOTES

Published in *Virginia Quarterly Review,* Spring 2005, special issue on Walt Whitman.

1. All quotations of Whitman are from *Leaves of Grass,* ed. Sculley Bradley and Harold W. Blodgett, Norton Critical Edition (New York: Norton, 1973).

2. Zygmunt Bauman, *Identity: Conversations with Benedetto Vecchi* (Malden, MA: Polity Press, 2004), 47.

3. Meena Alexander, *Raw Silk* (Evanston, IL: TriQuarterly Books, Northwestern University Press, 2004), 64–67.

4. Meena Alexander, *Shock of Arrival: Reflections on Postcolonial Experience* (Boston: South End Press, 1996), 1.

5. These lines are translated by the poet. The Malayalam original was first published in the weekly *Kalakaumudi,* April 1982, 24–25. The poem was included in Ayyappa Paniker, *Ayyappa Panikerude Kritikal, 1981–1989* (Kottayam, India: D. C. Books, 1989).

6. Personal communication, email, October 31, 2004, from Ayyappa Paniker.

7. Mattancherri Palace, also known as the Dutch Palace, was built by the Portugese in 1557 and gifted to the Kochi raja, Veera Kerala Varma. It was wrested away by the Dutch in 1663 and restored and expanded.

"The Shock of Sensation"

On Reading The Waves *as a Girl in India and a Woman in North America*

We have no ceremonies, only private dirges and no
conclusions, only violent sensations, each separate.
—Virginia Woolf, *The Waves*

I was young when I first read *The Waves*. I was in my grandmother Mariamma's bedroom in Kozencheri. The walls were
whitewashed, there were photographs of family, all over the
upper edge of the wall, broad foreheads, dark eyes peering
down, and in the single bookshelf to the right of grandmother's
bed, beneath the wooden cross, a motley array of English books
which did not belong to her, for my grandmother Mariamma
never read English books. Perhaps they had belonged to my
other grandmother, who loved English literature and had died
before I was born, or perhaps one or two of the books had come
from my father's collection. There they were stacked upright:
The Bible, a volume of Shakespeare, Tagore, H. G. Wells, Conan
Doyle, Dickens, Emily Brontë, and a copy of Virginia Woolf's
The Waves. I recall how I sat at the edge of the bed and pulled
The Waves off the shelf.

Before I opened the book I glanced out of the window. There
were no humans visible, but I could see the brown cow tugging
at its rope, nuzzling into sweet hay; a goat tipsy with heat; white
doves scrambling awkwardly toward the seeds in the dovecote,
hardly bothering to flap their wings. Life seemed suspended in
a heat haze. And grandmother herself, perhaps saying her
prayers in the next room, or supervising the cook as she made
sambar or coconut chutney, was nowhere to be seen. I thumbed
through the book, knocked dust off the bottom edge, then

opened the cool pages. As I buried my nose in the shining letters, I felt I was falling into water.

I had never before encountered prose that danced quite in that way, drawing me over the surface of shining particles, then tugging deep, deep to the gulf that underlies sense.

It was between the dark covers of that copy of *The Waves* that I first encountered the sense that truth could be verified by what was felt on the skin and in the bloodstream, that the body as Woolf put it "goes before me like a lantern down a dark lane, bringing one thing after another out of darkness into a ring of light."[1] This sense was critical to me, coming as it did as part of Woolf's notion of scattered bits and pieces, sensorial beckonings, of a "shattered mind which is pieced together by some sudden perception" (39). Reading *The Waves* I recognized in a deep, if unspoken awareness, a kindred spirit, one who took for granted the walls of old houses, ancestral gardens, the migrancy that time enforces.

By then I had spent so many years of my childhood traveling between India and North Africa. Starting from the age of five I had to learn to pack and unpack myself, accept that "reality," far from being solid, was singularly insubstantial, its loveliness could turn breathless in seconds. Solid walls could vanish, ancestral gardens could melt away. The sedimentation of the soul that I was starting to learn, my childhood and teenage years cut by border crossings, India and the Sudan the hundreds of miles of ocean or blue sky that layered them, drawing me into a difficult sense making, one I did not have a ready pattern for. What kind of creature was I if what I had known and loved, was always to be cut away, the passage of space casting veils over what the body had touched.

There was no simple narrative I could draw between the parts of my worlds. How could I speak of what I knew if the self could scarcely be taken for granted? And what might memory mean?

And holding a fresh copy of *The Waves* in my hand, for that old dark book in my grandmother's bedroom has vanished. I sit in my room in Manhattan, the green trees of summer outside my window.

I try to recall what sense I made of two figures, each no more than an outline, yet unfolding between them the whole tapestry of the book. One is a woman, the other a child. The woman maintains order by the sheer fact of her maturity, her stillness at the center of a bustling garden. She is "the lady" who "sits between two long windows writing" (17). She is as necessary to the growth of the garden as the men with their long brooms, sweeping. She calms the chaos, stills the fearful children. She does not look up from her writing. In my mind, she is linked to the poet in Wallace Stevens's poem "Mozart, 1935" with the haunting, troubling invocation: "poet be seated at the piano." Even if stones are thrown in the streets, or there are gunshots, riots outside the garden walls, the lady must maintain her seat, be wrapped in meditation, keep writing. It is she who keeps "reality," the word that Woolf puts to such fierce use at the end of *A Room of One's Own*.[2]

The other figure is that of the child, the girlchild cast out. Forced outside the loop of time, she starts to write. I will never forget the nervous thrill of reading the lines that follow, the origin of imaginative creation, but at the end, the writer herself, by her own hand, it would seem, forced out. What stringent necessity lay in this, what tragic foreshadowing of Virginia Woolf's end?

But we need to think beyond this, and ponder how these seeming fixities might be unlinked, how we might write beyond this ending.

"I begin to draw a figure and the world is looped in it, and I myself am outside the loop; which I now join—so—and seal up, and make entire. The world is entire and I am outside of it, crying, 'Oh, save me, from being blown forever outside the loop of time!'"[3]

Why should the writing child be flung outside the loop of time? Why should her hand tremble with fear as she writes? And how did she so painfully, so carefully acquire the discipline that turned her into the woman in the garden, writing?

The child is mother to the woman. I am only learning this now. What the child draws into the quick of her flesh is what the writing woman must etch into the lineaments of her landscape, her characters of knowledge, her tall green trees. But what kind of world does this woman inhabit? Must she forever be unhoused? I ponder Woolf's line: "my body passes vagrant as a bird's shadow" (66).

Her hold on the body was tenuous and puts me in mind of Wordsworth, whose Fenwick note to the Immortality Ode speaks of how as a child on his way to school, overcome by the sense of the unreality of all that was around, he put out his foot and touched a wall, a stone, tree to recall himself "from the abyss of idealism to reality." So too Woolf's speaker in *The Waves* who feels herself slip "into nothingness" and must bang her "hand against some hard door to call herself back to the body" (44).

But perhaps it was this very dissolution of the bodily hold on things that allowed for the textured layering of spaces, sharp and disjunctive sensations, that wrapping themselves, one over the other, could free the woman writer from an imprisoning social world. And if the simple self is set at risk, then that too forces a recognition of its impossible nature. There is nowhere one can simply be:

> This is the first day of a new life, another spoke of the rising wheel. But my body passes vagrant as a bird's shadow . . . I coerce my brain to form in my forehead; I force myself to state, if only in one line of unwritten poetry, this moment; to mark this inch in the long, long history that began in Egypt, in the time of the Pharoahs when women carried red pitchers to the Nile. I seem already to have lived many thousand years. But . . . I sit in a third-class railway carriage full of boys going home for the holidays. (66)

Reading these lines again, at a time of mass migrations, transnational crossings, gendered postcolonial reflections, I realize how my reading of *The Waves* quickened my girl's mind, a mind in search of form. The sharp disjunctions of space, the shock of motion, the edginess of sensation, even a violence to it so that the self can scarcely discover an underlying continuity in the flow of consciousness, all this sparked a quick recognition in me.

And where did that recognition lead me? I sense now, how close to me, how buried under my own skin was my own reading of Virginia Woolf's "flaw" in creation, a crack in the world

(25). How her fear of even stepping over a puddle, or of what the looking glass might reveal, reverberates in me. And always on the other side is the civilized world, others who are "immaculate," watching, staring. The sense of a fault in things, of a broken, fissured earth courses through my poetry and prose. A few years ago I published a memoir called *Fault Lines*. In it I try to reflect on the ways in which my being here, in America, is underwritten by multiple border crossings, languages, voices. I try to write out a palimpsest of memory without which the present could not exist. In this way, each moment of reflection becomes a threshold. Though Virginia Woolf in no way entered consciously into my mind as I wrote *Fault Lines* it seems to me now, in hindsight, that Woolf's influence on me, rich and subterranean, was all the more intense for being hidden. So that while I had read and even taught *Mrs Dalloway* and *To the Lighthouse* to my students at Hunter College and used Woolf's essays in my work *Women in Romanticism,* never ever had I alluded to the one book that had marked me so deep, so early.[4] Something kept me away from *The Waves,* a dark shadow, a hand.

But *The Waves* was the work I drank so deeply of, in the whitewashed room in my paternal grandmother's house, a house with lime trees outside the window, the footmarks of an baby elephant, its round gray body and sinuous trunk puffing dirt, bits of broken leaf, all night, in the lower garden in an attempt to cool itself. As the lines of *The Waves* turned in my head, the snorting sounds of the baby elephant drifted up to me, and when I looked through my parents' window I could see its dark shadow, gray, humped in between the mango trees and the rubber trees.

But what happened to me when I could no longer see the baby elephant? When the "I" that saw the elephant no longer existed? Forced dislocations made a simple narrative—and then and then and then—hard, even untenable for me.

These days, I am engaged in my usual practice: in between poems, scribbling prose, the chaos of identity just about balanced by the edginess of aesthetic form, the one and the other always entwined for me as the questions continue to haunt me: Who am I? Where am I? When am I? Again and again I feel as if I were forced to start from scratch, all over again making up both self and world. And I need to ask, how did Virginia Woolf, in the early years of the twentieth century, have such a vivid sense of dislocation, living as she seems to have done, so close to home? Could it be, that over and above the physical facts of migrancy, there is an essential condition that etches itself into visibility through traumatic loss? No quick answer is possible.

Perhaps this was why *The Waves* spoke to me, in the many voices of an English woman who had never traveled very far from home, a great and difficult writer, her soul marked by inner motion, speed unsettling a psyche that deliberately maintained the most tenuous hold on its bodily station, all the better to underwrite a language of fraught, bejeweled sensation.

And there it lies, right at the heart of the modernist enterprise, I tell myself, Woolf's writing, a glistening palimpsest of bodily knowledge, a body of work immensely useful to a postcolonial imagination in search of dissolving structures.

But something else has to be spelt out, as crucial as right hand is to left, given the integrity of the body, or left foot to right, for one who would seek out her own mobility in the realm of letters. My early awareness of Woolf's power, and my love of her writing, was cut by another emotion in me, a distinct refusal, a rage at the white, colonial world in which she lived, moved, and had her being.

How could I doubt that I would forever be part of that "Oriental problem" she alluded to in *The Waves*, the dark poor world Percival was riding into, the world of those who were pitiful and did not speak good English. And didn't she write of how the "violent language" that Percival uses to solve the problem might set things right (136). If I sensed the irony in Woolf's tone, it cut no ice with me, for I was clear on which side she stood, the side of those Gandhi had struggled against, those to whom India would forever be a series of flat pictures, depicting dark natives, painted dancers, mud, heat, dust, all the "fragility and decay" of a lesser ontology, an elsewhere that could never compete with the English present, an India that was illusory, never amounting to more than "temporarily run up buildings in some Oriental exhibition" (136). And while she had the flow of English, and bathed in the river of the language, I was forever cast to the rocky shores, my feet cut by the sharp stones, jagged syllables I was forced to repeat over and over again by my British tutor: "cut," "cut," "mutt," "mutt," the violence of a colonial pedagogy, its sense of utter rightness, of one world, one Empire, hurting my child's mind, making me recoil from the very language I needed to live and breathe and move in as a writer.

Then too the storybooks my tutor gave me—this British woman my parents found to teach me when we traveled to North Africa—had pages filled with little white children who wore pinafores and had pink cheeks and drank milk and ate muffins. I had no doubt that had they caught sight of me, or of my grandmother Mariamma, they would have run a mile, perhaps hidden out in their bungalows. Or cried out to their soldiers to come and push me back into the jungle where I belonged. And as a girl I had no doubt that Virginia Woolf, for all her anguish, all her resistance, came from that very British world. The avowal, indeed the complicated truth, that each and every one of us is part of a historical moment and must bear its burdens could not in any way have eased what I felt.

And so the affiliation with a foremother was cut by the sense of disenfranchisement, the awareness of a racialized world which would force my own body into the shadows, into the bushes, away from the "immaculate others." And this in spite of, perhaps even intensified by, the fact that Woolf herself understood what it meant to be robbed of identity.

So the layered, sedimented worlds, the opposite histories from which we came, the density of the whiteness that clung to her, invaded me. And later, in the years that I was studying the writings of Mary Wollstonecraft, I felt that by casting aside her own rage, exiling it in works like *Three Guineas* and *A Room of One's Own*, Virginia Woolf was whitewashing her fiction, paying too heavy a price for the exquisite fabric of sensation. And there were years when I did not read her work, could not read her work.

In the past few months, I feel I have reached a watershed in my own writing life, a period when after intense labor I can stop, turn back, reflect on what has entered into the texture of writing, what has gone into the making of my visible world. I realize now my deep indebtedness to Woolf, to the ways in which she etches in the strangeness that lies just under the surface of our skin and I see shadows pinned under doves that circle slowly to the dovecote, in an ancient garden I no longer return to.

In my room in New York City, thousands of miles from that garden, ever so slowly I murmur her lines again: "The structure is visible. We have made a dwelling" (164).

And the dwelling is one made of words, words of a colonial language I have stripped and polished down and torn apart with my own hands so that the homeless voices of my generation can enter in.

I tried my hand at a novel, first one and then another. *Manhattan Music* focuses on the life of an Indian woman haunted by her memories of the past. Sandhya, an immigrant, tries to adjust to life in the new world. During the Gulf War she goes to an antiwar protest and, listening to descriptions of ongoing bombardment, she senses her own mind at the brink of disintegration. Voices pour through her. The body is pitched against its own need to simply have and hold onto the ordinary world and can barely shelter these homeless voices. It is only at the very end of the novel that Sandhya is able to walk freely into the city, filled with a sense that she can survive the present.[5]

In my need to braid in these voices, I have taken what I could from Virginia Woolf. And if she were to hear them and clapping her hands over her ears, turn away, sensing nothing but the dark crudity of a face that peers in over the shoulder, invading the gilt-framed mirror, then let that too, be part of our story, part of our lives in a postcolonial theater, a world cut from ancient ceremonies, filled with what Woolf once called "the shock of sensation" (130):

> Voices stirred . . . drawing her down to a rough basement—a dark, muddy place where syllables stirred their moist roots.
>
> She heard her sister Nunu cry out in the Sanskrit her tutor forced on her: "*Aham patashala getchami!*" the singsong of recitation. She heard Arabic from the lyrics Rashid learned from his mother, a burial song, a woman with a swanlike neck, exiled in life, returned to her native soil in death. She heard voices from the streets of Bosnia, Rwanda, Sri Lanka, strange countries bruised as plums might be in a gunny sack.

Voices too, from mats and torn mattresses stained with virginal blood, moans and sharp cries of pleasure, exhalations of delight.

These sounds played within her in a ceaseless cacophony, struggling to become speech: the homeless voices of Sandhya Maria Rosenblum.

NOTES

Published in *Meridians: Feminism, Race, Transnationalism,* Spring 2001 inaugural issue.

1. Virginia Woolf, *The Waves* (New York: Harcourt Brace, 1959), 129. Subsequent references to *The Waves* are given in the text.
2. Virginia Woolf, *A Room of One's Own* (New York: Harcourt Brace, 1957), 113–14.
3. Meena Alexander, *Fault Lines* (New York: Feminist Press, 1993). For an elaboration of memory as a threshold "that deepens what it is that migration or dislocation does," see the interview in which I speak of this: "Gold Horizon: The Unquiet Borders of Memory," in Eileen Tabios, *Black Lightning: Poetry in Progress* (New York: Asian American Writers Workshop, 1998), 195–226.
4. Meena Alexander, *Women in Romanticism: Mary Wollstonecraft, Dorothy Wordsworth, and Mary Shelley* (London: Macmillan, 1989). See the chapter entitled "Natural Enclosures."
5. Meena Alexander, *Manhattan Music* (San Francisco: Mercury House, 1997), 193. For related questions of self-identity and border crossings, see "Rites of Passage," in this volume.

Poetry of Decreation

Twilight in Cuttack. The wind barely rustles in the dry leaves. A man lifts his hand, his head bent, listening. For almost an eternity he stands, as the wind blows, swiftly now, through the dry leaves and sifts the green pointed twigs on the tree. Quickly, his hand in consort with the wind, he parts the dark mesh of leaf just above his head. How silently he beckons! In the glow of torchlight I see the pointed twigs bent in a round, the tiny freckled eggs, warm, almost smoky. He drops his hand and the leaves cover the nest. It is dark now in Cuttack, the wind dying in the shadows, in the soil.

The image remains with me. It was Jayanta Mahapatra showing me the koil's nest. I choose to begin with this memory for the quality of attentiveness it discloses, the absolute inclination to the movement of the wind so that the nest is not unnaturally disturbed, the care for a secret being.

This patience, this quality of attention which is the finest refinement of desire distinguishes the work of Jayanta Mahapatra, a remarkable poet, writing now, in English in India. In a tongue which is not that of his mother, yet which he has made his own, he establishes a fragile self, waiting, "listening, pinned to the stone." Stone is crucial to Mahapatra's cosmogony. It was there at the beginning. It is the penetrable permanent. He inhabits an earth where monuments of stone crumble and crack, yet survive in the same realm as human beings, the glory of stone glimpsed by consciousness. Stone does not vanish as flesh does, yet to reach the still point it must be transcended just as the self must be emptied out.

In a poem called "The Ruins" he alludes to the pain of stone, cracked by time:

> Chipped fingers, the thin crack
> running slant along the brow.

A tragic tone is released: "so like a word, its blue wings broken." Yet we, speaker and listener, both using words, are bound to this ruin. Language fails us, even as we struggle to understand. The flaw lies in our very being, in the way in which we inhere in this world, pitted by time:

> Nothing that is whole
> speaks of the past. Or lives.
> Or can form into a word.[1]

Simone Weil, the great French religious thinker, has spoken of decreation as a certain quality of attention, an emptying out of the self, an almost mystical waiting. She argues that it requires giving up "our imaginary position as the center, to renounce it, not only intellectually but in the imaginative part of the soul." Annihilation of what we normally call identity, a position at the center of space, works a change in the very quality of perception

> A transformation then takes place at the very roots of our sensibility . . . analogous to that which takes place in the dusk of an evening on a road, where we suddenly recognize as a rustling of leaves what we thought at first was whispering voices. We see the same colors; we hear the same sounds, but not in the same way.[2]

It is precisely this painful transformation, a withdrawal of the will, the power of a visionary consciousness filling up the place the will had bent to its own purposes, that we see in Mahapatra's poetry. Even the human body vanishes, giving up the centrality of location it had maintained. But what happens next? The mind is gently consumed, from the edges, inwards.

> With his body, he loses body,
> pales into a place.
> Nothing matters,
> the river grows,
> the hill takes a high face.

This mystic light oozes everywhere,

                                           like sweat.

Absorbing, it eats his mind
slowly around the edges.

The "mystic light" is the visible aspect of time, and the self will
vanish into its depths. This is not the Romantic figuration of consciousness expanding. Rather, Mahapatra confronts the issue of
identity that arises for each and every writer in India, the anguished need to define a self, out of the bottomless flow of time;
to cut identity out of the "sky's eternal vault."[3] For the poet, un-
like the mystic, must continually, perilously, return to the realms
of individuation; travel the journey back and forth, ceaselessly. In
his long poem *Relationship* Mahapatra meditates on the problem
of a self, overwhelmed by time. He seeks "a prayer to draw my
body out of a thousand years." Yet the poet must still persevere,
search "time's mouth" till finally the realization dawns on him:
the utterance is silence.

> But time has no mouth,
> and the black labyrinth
> of casurinas along the edges of the sea
> closes the sky's eternal vault . . .[4]

In his 1976 volume *A Father's Hours,* in a poem entitled "The
Twentyfifth Anniversary of a Republic, 1975" the poet had ex-
plored the visionary silence of a holy man who sits under a
brand new awning in the marketplace. Children, their bodies
like "rough-hewn stone," go up to him. The speaker strains to
hear their words, but he fails. Darkness falls:

> I leaned forward and touched the man's still shoulder.
> Cruelties trickled like insensible resin
> from his torn wounded trunk.
> The centuries locked like wheels.[5]

The entire memory of a race is locked into flesh, fragile,
vulnerable to touch, yet curiously permanent, like stone. The
old man's body is porous, like ancient stone, taking on the
knowledge of a soil, of buried dreams and myths. Yet his flesh is
eternally wounded.

It is the wound of poetry, the gash in the body when the body is lent to the soil. Yet out of suffering the true word emerges, trembling at the brink of darkness. Paradoxically, it is utterly lucid, clarified by the light of vision, by a self that is one with the soil in which it finds itself:

> The distant music of the stars cuts blood
> and the suffering of the earth returns.

I think of the Finnish poet Paavo Haavikko, a writer of intense clarity, his speech refined by ice and snow, by

> The journey through familiar speech
> towards the region that is no place.[6]

With Mahapatra, a writer as luminous as Haavikko, the journey is only intermittently toward "the region that is no place." Mahapatra has chosen a difficult task. What time splinters must continually be remade, the world recast again and again from consciousness. At the culmination of *Relationship* we hear him say: "I draw the day unto myself, trembling with being." And in a poem called "The Mountain" he writes of the gravity of a mountain continually sifting, chopping, splintering under the pressure of attention:

> Shackled to earth it stands, all its dead weight.
> In the darkness of evening
> silence and pressure only,
> multiplying, adding, subtracting,
> in the abyssal heart.
> Each day,
> falling to pieces under the straddling sunlight,
> it gives clear proof that one
> might still reconstruct one's life . . .[7]

We have a powerful, haunting image of the world made and remade through the visionary instinct. But this is not to say that there is a real solid self. That would be too simple a way out. Poetry comes when a soil speaks, when time is "broken into small fragments of light and shadow." The voice comes from a realm beyond the common self, pierced by "a too true transience."

But this is no common soil, no ordinary earth; in Mahapatra's world "the trembling of dreams is everywhere, like the wind."

In his "Orissa Journal" Mahapatra speaks of the source of dream, of memories that "flit like clouds in the sky."[8] After detailed description of an encounter with Govinda Maharana, the local image maker who knows he must shape the goddess Durga both as creator and destroyer, the speaker moves to a reflection on the crowded noisy festivities and embedded in the teeming soil, the cosmic spark, life, that as the *Upanishads* tells him springs from the smoke of desire. "For a moment," says the speaker, "I forget myself . . . I hold my breath":

> The physical perspective changes every moment; perhaps this is what hammers on the shell of one's inherent isolation, that time is not constant, and the present is not the present any longer. Slowly I realize that I am living at one particular instant in many layers of time—the mythic, the historical and the present. What one sees in the present is only what has stirred the air of the place for countless generations.

In such a world, which is truly India, the gesture of grace involves an attentive waiting; emptying out the self, waiting, watching, witnessing. The largest untruth would be the imposition of will, positing a solid central self. In one of his finest poems, "The Abandoned British Cemetery at Balasore, India," Mahapatra gives us the resigned, meditative poise needed to survive in such a world. The British conquerors have vanished, leaving their tombs behind, haunt now of lizard and scorpion. The terror of mutability is upon the self and there is no escape. The young are dying; they reflect the "blood's unease," and "death's sickly trickle" is everywhere, gathering power and momentum:

> through both past and present, the increasing young,
> into the final bone, wearying all truth with ruin.
> This is the iron
>
> rusting in the vanquished country, the blood's unease,
> the useless rain upon my familiar window . . .[9]

What becomes of the bond between death and the self? Death is a birthright and must be drawn into the voice; into the source of power. "The age old grass of my death," the poet calls it in *Relationship,* echoing the "tribe of grass in the cracks of my eyes" in "The Abandoned British Cemetery." For it is only when death is evoked that the beginning will give itself up, the "ruined birthplace" appear and the voice reach the final fragrance, the fragrance from the one bloom absent from all bouquets.

In his long poem, Mahapatra speaks of those who are able to live with the knowledge of death, beyond the myth of happiness. It is a cold, sparse landscape of the mind:

> I thought: those who survive the myth
> have slipped past their lives and cannot define their reason,
> the trees are getting sparse, the clouds dwindle into colder
> air . . .

But it is this realm and no other that holds "the open center of the heart's space." Here we are given solitude, the limpid truth of "something hatching alone on the unknown leaf." It is a realm of beginnings, a tenuous redemption, a truth for the mind unwearied by time. A poet one is truly grateful for, Mahapatra shows us the quivering movement out of darkness:

> a vine climbing silently in space
> or emerging through strange water,
> reedy and naked and of death.

The poetry of decreation has come full circle. Out of the "silent alphabet of belief" has emerged a new world; for the posture of grace, a vine, climbing up through "strange water."

NOTES

Published in the *Journal of Commonwealth Literature* 18, no. 1 (1983): 42–47.

1. Jayanta Mahapatra, *A Rain of Rites* (Athens: University of Georgia Press, 1976), 36.

2. Simone Weil, *Waiting for God*, trans. Emma Craufurd (New York: G. P. Putnam's, 1951), 159.

3. Jayanta Mahapatra, *Relationship* (Greenfield Center, NY: Greenfield Review Press, 1980), 10.

4. Mahapatra, *Relationship*, 10.

5. Jayanta Mahapatra, *A Father's Hours* (Calcutta: United Writers, 1976), 26.

6. Paavo Haavikko, *Selected Poems* (Harmondsworth: Penguin, 1974), 51.

7. Jayanta Mahapatra, *The False Start* (Bombay: Clearing House, 1980), 41.

8. Jayanta Mahapatra, "An Orissa Journal: July to November 1972," *Queens's Quarterly* 80, no. 1 (1973): 66.

9. Mahapatra, *The False Start*, 71.

II. Picturing Sense

Pitching a Tent

1. Poetry makes a dwelling for us, a tent of words.
2. The tent has holes for the wind to blow through, holes pierced by gunfire, by arrows, by sharp stones.
3. It can be pitched on solid ground, or rolled up, borne through air, carried over water. It can be unfurled here or there.
4. Inside the shelter we turn from the violence of history, to the lyric measures of poetry, so that we can see again, eyes wiped free of blood; so that we can hear again, the voices that allow us to be human.
5. Poetry makes ground in a vertiginous world.
6. All this is true, and necessary for our survival.
7. None of this is true.

Unquiet Borders

The unquiet borders of poetry: I muse on Mirabai,[1] poet mystic of the bhakti movement in India, she who left home and princely husband and roved across thresholds, borders. She left behind her the confines of domesticity. Her saris were torn; her hair matted, lacking the oil that Indian women prize. Her feet were dry, chapped. And she roved; she sang of Krishna continually, that perpetual absent, her beloved. Was Mira's body covered with dirt, like that of Akkamahadevi, another great woman poet, such that she might have been said to wear a skin of dirt? And what of menstrual blood? How did she wash it off? Or did it mix in with the mud?

I ask all this quite deliberately, here, now, on this North American continent. I ask: What would it mean if Mirabai were alive, here, now, in America? How would she write? What sense would the world we inhabit make to her?

I will try and answer by pretending I can see into her soul. We poets do that a lot and failing, stand dismayed at our own shortfalls. Still, first her body. She let her body show. It was warm in Rajasthan in most seasons. Her skin was brown. It was not enough, crouched in the hot alleyway, to sing of Krishna (*I am your knife, you my noose*), to sing of palaces that did not offer food for the soul. She lived in dirt shacks, wandered over soiled thresholds.

She crossed a border, never to return. I imagine her, here, now. But what do they make of her, a brown-skinned woman in tattered oriental clothing at the edge of Broadway? Or perhaps she is wandering by the railroad tracks in New Brunswick. Or is she hunched on the sidewalk, or rooting in the garbage for food?

Then again, we might find Mira, like many other immigrant

women, working in a sweatshop on the Lower East Side, the rhythms of her poetry beaten to the tracking needle, silks spinning out of her skin, English syllables edgy, forced, *brajbhasha* flowering only in dreams. The hidden language that flowers only in dreams torn from the body.

Frantz Fanon, whom Mirabai did not need to read (in his work, women are so much cast aside), in a crucial section of *Black Skins, White Masks,* imagines people crying out, "Look, a Negro!" So she might find the fingers pointing: "Look, a brown woman!" The shame, the torment, the turning, beseeching others. Stumbling, falling, the body splintering into a thousand shards. The body split open. "I burst apart," Fanon writes. "Now the fragments have been put together again by another self."[2]

What is this other self? What might this putting together of a racialized body mean? A body not male, but female, haunted by its femaleness, earth it cannot shed. Will Krishna put her together again? Or is this the secret of her genius—the impossible sense that Krishna, who lies in wait for her under the waters of sleep, will not stitch her back together again, piece together the broken bits? So who will put together a body torn by border crossings, skin marked by barbed wire, bandages hastily knotted, the body of a pariah woman?

Why do I conceive of the female poet this way? Perhaps because I think that she needs to slip out of her flesh in order to sing, yet it is only by being drawn back into a larger, more spiritual body, the mouths of many others, the hands that labor in the sweatshops, on the street corners, in the marketplaces, and, yes, in the academies, that she can write.

Our world is filled with unquiet borders. It would be an error— too grave to be borne—to think that our capacity for words must cross out our bodies. Bodies banned, beaten, jailed, twisted in childbirth; bodies that are the sites of pleasure, of ecstasy. Female bodies that can babble, break into prophetic speech, rant.

Any aesthetic implications? I hear someone ask. None, except what I have called elsewhere a "back against the wall aesthetic."[3] The woman poet who faces the borders her body must cross, racial and sexual borders, is forced to invent a form that springs out without canonical support, a rough-and-ready thing, its order crude, its necessity beyond the purchase of self-invention. There is something here in the body, in pain or pleasure, crying out for a sense that we need to attend to.

I try to learn from Mirabai, from her nakedness. The most delicate play of words is what we aspire to in the face of what confronts us. The beloved perpetually lost, the body fragmented, its bits and pieces spelling out a map that a poet might make, crossing unquiet borders.

NOTES

Published in *Crab Orchard Review,* special issue on Asian American literature, 3, no. 2 (Spring–Summer 1998). A version of this essay was originally presented at the roundtable "Poetry, Feminism and the Difficult World," at the conference "Poetry and the Public World," Rutgers University, April 26, 1997.

1. Mirabai, c. 1498–1565, of royal descent, left hearth and home to wander abroad, singing the praises of Krishna. She is considered one of the major figures of the devotional movement of bhakti, in which love of the deity often takes intense, erotic form. Mirabai wrote in both Gujarati and Brajbhasa, the latter a dialect of Hindi in which a great deal of devotional poetry was composed.

2. Frantz Fanon, *Black Skin, White Masks,* trans. Charles Lam Markmann (New York: Grove Press, 1967), 109.

3. Meena Alexander, "Skin with Fire Inside: Indian Women Writers," in *The Shock of Arrival: Reflections on Postcolonial Experience* (Boston: South End Press, 1996), 170.

Rights of Passage

There is something I have to deal with in terms of the postcolonial. It presses on me, in the way that a pen point might, thrust inadvertently into the palm; or it turns, a hot flash in a dream that leaves an aftertaste in the mouth, something fiery, but with no readily discernable shape. So words must be worked, to make sense, and the skin of the taken-for-granted turned inside out.

"Aren't you a postcolonial writer?"

Now, that is a fairly innocent question, surely nothing a self-respecting woman would want to deny. It seems to me that I have been asked that question fairly recently, but in the hearing of it—at least for the part of the self that tries to string thoughts out in some measured discourse, as opposed to the razzmatazz logic of a poem—something skids, blurs.

I hear a splatter of other questions. I am sitting in Keshari Memorial Hall in Tiruvananthapuram, Kerala. Outside, on the street, the rain beats down, a gentle rain, damp and warm, such as I have grown accustomed to from childhood. I am in a press conference being asked questions. All sorts of questions. Then comes: "Aren't you a left-leaning writer?" Tired of sitting still and facing so many questions, I pitch in my seat, all the way to the left, and in the sudden laughter, try to piece together an answer. I have never been a member of any political party. Yes, I am concerned with issues of social justice; yes, I do have my sympathies. Then comes a request that I read "Ashtamudi Lake," a poem that has come out in Malayalam translation. This is more comfortable territory, to enter into the lilt of a poem one has made and forgotten, leave aside the rocky terrain of labeling: Who are you? What are you? When are you?

I read lines about the train plunging into the lake, the deafening clap of waters, the rusty carriages dragged out. Then comes another question: "Are you a feminist writer?" I take my time with that one, sit up in the seat and keep quiet for what seems a long while. No one interrupts. Feminism has been very important to me. So much of what I write about would have been cut from me if it weren't for the questions that feminism has raised, about a woman's body, woman's writing. I have learned to think through feminism, I say. I am a feminist, yes. But a feminist writer? No. And the distinction is very important to me. I try to speak a little of my belief that one should stand at the barricades, march in the streets. But in the brief quiet of a space in which to write, even the construction of the barricades, or the street in which one marches, should be drawn up again, questioned, flooded with the inchoate, often mute emotion that makes us what we are.

I was back in Manhattan by the time the weekend papers carried the account. My sister, who was in Kerala at the time visiting from Madras, said to me, "You have gone straight to every middle-class Malayali's heart." I ask her what she means. "There's a large spread here in the Arts Section," she says, "with an account of the press conference, and it has you saying, 'I am not a feminist.'"

"But I didn't say that."

"What did you say?" she asks.

So over again, on the phone, I speak of what I have said. "I do believe in women's protests, in the right to struggle in the public world, you know that," I tell her, and so our conversation continues. Outside my window I hear the rain, so much colder here in the fall, but as the drops splatter against the window, I ponder the jagged geographies of our lives, the worth of words, harsh migrancies.

This brings me back to the questions posed in the editorial statement I was sent, and for good measure I toss in another and imagine being asked, "Aren't you a postcolonial writer?" Should I tilt sharply to the left, draw laughter? Keep a wise silence?

In some ways the answer is crystal clear. History answers for me. Born in Allahabad a few years after Indian independence, what else should I be? I grew up partly in the Sudan, a country that had just gained its independence from Britain. I learned to write my poems in English, a postcolonial language. But these statements cover over a complexity, something having to do with the flesh of words. I use that phrase because I don't know how else to put it.

The flesh of words. There are some poems that are like bits of armor to me, postcolonial poems. "Brown Skin, What Mask?" is like that.

Brown Skin, What Mask?

Babel's township seeps into Central Park
I hunch on a stone bench scraping nightingale-bulbuls
cuckoo-koels, rose-gulabs off my face

No flim-flam now; card sharp, street wise
I fix my heels at Paul's Shoe Place for a dollar fifty
get a free make-over at Macy's, eyes smart, lips shine.
Shall I be a hyphenated thing, Macaulay's Minutes
and Melting Pot theories not withstanding?

Shall I shall bruise my skin, burn up into
She Who Is No Color whose longing is a crush
of larks shivering without sound?

When lit by his touch in a public place
—an elevator with a metal face—shall I finger grief for luck
work stares into the "bride is never naked" stuff?

I wrote the poem, published it in a journal and then in a collection of my poems, and then gave it away. I gave it away to a male character in my novel *Manhattan Music*. The character is called Jay for short, Arjun Sankaramangalam for long. He's an Indian photographer who took shots of civil unrest, riots, the pogroms against the Sikhs in Sultanpuri. One of his photos, of a dumb child with his hands outstretched, makes him famous. He leaves India, stumbles into Manhattan, finds he can no longer take photographs. The frame doesn't work; he can't compose his shots. He wraps his camera in a bit of green silk, puts it in a closet, and then the poems start. Little bitsy poems, and they trouble him. They come in a woman's voice, it seems. Why write poetry? his friends say. How many people read a poem? Two, three if you're lucky. What's happened to your photos? But Jay can't help himself. He reads his poems to anyone

who will listen. One of his friends, sitting in a bar, tells him off:
The poem about brown skins, is much too drab, too wordy. The
poem as armor, the postcolonial poem—I wanted to give it away.
I did not want to carry it about any more, have it be mine. Too
much of a strain.

Then there are other poems that are like flesh, the vulnerable
part. For me, no labels attach to them. A poem like "House of a
Thousand Doors" is in a woman's voice and set on the Kerala
coast; another I have just finished, called "Rites of Sense," is in a
daughter's voice. It makes no sense to me to call them postcolonial; they are so personal to me. They come out of a wordless
part of the psyche, the part that didn't learn the rules of language very well. The last lines of "Rites of Sense," speaking of my
mother, go like this:

> [You] taught me to fire a copper pan
> starch and fold a sari, raise a rusty needle,
> stitch my woman's breath
> into the mute amazement / of sentences.

Although I feel this distinction in what I have written, in my
self-understanding, as it were, it surely does not mean I am two
sorts of writer: postcolonial and not. And how helpful are such
questions? Why make trouble for myself? I think. Yet the trouble
these questions raise has to do with territory, psychic territory,
and with the migrations of sense. All part and parcel of a postcolonial world—and here I lay claim to that hard adjective,
mindful of the difficulty it can bring. I cannot forget the unex-
pected attack a year ago when my book of essays, *The Shock of
Arrival,* came out, with the subtitle *Reflections on Postcolonial
Experience.* A previously sympathetic critic accused me of falling
into "poco correctness," of using the dreaded word in order to
gain acceptance. I longed to raise my arms, let all the words flow
off like quiet monsoon rain. But I finally wrote to him: These
cross-hatchings, these migrant mappings are part of my biogra-
phy, they're not just imaginary inventions. These fault lines
make up my world.

To conclude, I need to wander away a little: Awhile back I was
in Johannesburg, at the "Trade Routes and Diasporas" confer-

ence that took place as part of the city's Biennale. It was the first time I had been to Africa since I had left at the age of eighteen to go to university in Britain. In the plane flying over from Berlin, I kept rereading parts of Gandhi's *Autobiography*. I wanted to hold onto those pages. I wanted to puzzle out something that had haunted me for ever so long, how Gandhi—without whom there would be no postcolonial India as we know it— had been marked by his own migratory passages. How the telling humiliation of the pass laws in South Africa, the growing awareness of being a racialized body, allowed him to understand the horror of Untouchability in India. After all, it was the same man, same skin, same body, the same vital, brooding subjectivity, the same fraught spiritual economy crossing and recrossing the black waters.

During the panel—where I began with a few words on reading Gandhi—I spoke on a subject I had set myself. It seemed fluid, mellifluous, part of the unbroken rhythm of the inner life. I had titled the presentation "Translated Lives: The Poetry of Migration."

That afternoon there was some free time and a lull in the crowds trying to get into one of the main exhibition halls, in Newtown Cultural Precinct. I decided to try my luck. I made my way slowly through the outer metal doors of the hall. It had once been an immense workshop for electricity, the old-fashioned kind complete with huge pipes and boilers and pistons, refitted for the Biennale as an immense installation space. I approached the inner entrance and was confronted by two guards—young black men dressed in uniforms, complete with peaked caps and shining badges. I stepped forward. After all, I had my badge, which, even if handwritten, clearly said "Conference Delegate." One of them shoved his face right into mine, put his arm out. I stepped back, shaken. The other was a foot away, watching intently.

"Where is your pass?" asked the watching man.

"Pass?" I pointed at my badge. He shook his head. I couldn't believe what was happening. Had time slipped back in Johannesburg?

"Madam, this way please," said the rougher, ruder guard, and I backed away, forced to follow him. There was someone seated at a table. "There, you need an ID card."

"ID?"

"Yes, a pass card to enter."

The sense of something quite unreal hit me. I stared at the guard at the desk. Who was it? I moved closer to her.

"You're Meena, aren't you?" she said.

"Yes." I was relieved but confused.

"You know me?"

"Yes, I've read your work."

Someone was going to bail me out. The panic that had slipped up in me, making it just that little bit harder to breathe, started to ease. It was a woman facing me, though dressed in guard's uniform. She put out her hand. "Hi, I'm Coco!"

"Coco Fusco?"

"Right!"

I was thrilled to see her, the New York City performance artist.

"I was scared you know, really," I confessed to her, half laughing as I entered the booth to have my photo taken and she pasted it into the passbook and signed it for me. "Always expecting somewhere, deep down, to be stopped, denied entry."

"That's why I'm doing this performance," she said. "Its called 'Rights of Passage.'"

"And the guards?"

"Sure, they're kids, we pay them to act the part."

Later I realized how foolish I had been to panic that way, but I could not forget the fear—almost a lost instinct, but surely there, deep down in the buried part of the heart. A young artist at the Biennale, a South African Indian, later said to me, "You know, the white people who're stopped, they get really angry, but people like us get scared. Yes, scared. Why?"

"Why do you think?"

"It feels real. That's why, man!"

NOTE

Published in *Interventions: The International Journal of Postcolonial Studies* 1, no. 1 (1998), inaugural issue.

An Intimate Violence

There is a painful edge to the word *race*. Sometimes I cannot help thinking of it as a wound, something that cannot be cleft apart from my femaleness. And yet, at the same time, when I step back a little, there is the sense that race is an illusion, something made up. Otherwise why would I be so different in different places—by which I mean seen differently, treated differently, almost becoming another *I*? So it is that when crossing borders—between India and America, or even between the rich multiethnic mix of New York and the white suburbs—I feel a transitoriness in the self, the need for a febrile translation. And somehow there is a violent edge to this process of cultural translation, the shifting worlds I inhabit, the borders I cross in my dreams, the poems I make.

I was giving a reading in Cambridge, Massachusetts, in a bookstore. I read prose pieces, poems, ending with the last two sections of the poem "San Andreas Fault." A woman raised her hand. She picked out details from the poem: "How can you allow these facts of the world, terrible things we would not normally want to think about, get into your poem? What does it do to your life?"

Quiet for a bit, I took a while to respond, musing on the section of the poem she had picked out. It begins with a speaker, a woman, who enters a dream state. At the end of her vision she faces her muse, a weightless creature, born of air, who has forced her to this:

Late at night in Half Moon Bay
hair loosed to the glow of traffic lights
I slit the moist package of my dreams.

Female still, quite metamorphic
I flowed into Kali ivory tongued, skulls nippling my breasts
Durga lips etched with wires astride an electric tiger
Draupadi born of flame betrayed by five brothers stripped
of silks in the banquet hall of shame.

In the ghostly light of those women's eyes
I saw the death camps at our century's end:

A woman in Sarajevo shot to death
as she stood pleading for a pot of milk,
a scrap of bread, her red scarf swollen
with lead hung in a cherry tree.

Turks burnt alive in the new Germany,
a grandmother and two girls
cheeks puffed with smoke
as they slept in striped blankets
bought new to keep out the cold.

A man and his wife in Omdurman
locked to a starving child, the bone's right
to have and hold never to be denied,
hunger stamping the light.

In Ayodhya, in Ram's golden name
hundreds hacked to death, the domes
of Babri Masjid quivering as massacres begin—
the rivers of India rise mountainous,
white veils of the dead, dhotis, kurtas, saris,
slippery with spray, eased from their bloodiness.

Shaking when I stopped I caught myself short
firmly faced her "What forgiveness here?"
"None" she replied "Every angel knows this.
The damage will not cease and this sweet gorge
by which you stand bears witness.

Become like me a creature of this fault."[1]

  She was in the back of the room, a small, neat-looking woman,
her brown hair drawn back, and she was waiting for an answer.
  "There are two things," I began, "and they stand apart, then
come together. One is the music of poetry. Not something I am
altogether conscious about, but it works with the language, and

it allows the thoughts, the 'facts' if you will—the terror, the violence—to be raised up, so that even as we see them imprinted in consciousness, there is a hairbreadth that allows release, allows for the transcendence poetry seeks.

"Then my personal life." At this I stopped, took a sip of water, looked around the small room, the faces listening intently, the windows with the white shutters letting in a pearly light. The shutters looked as if they were cut from rice paper. Outside was spring sunshine, magnolias on the brink of bursting into light, crocuses prickling through the grass, spurts of purple among the old parked cars, the gas station on the other side of Hampshire Road.

I took courage from all that lay around and the women and men listening in the small back room.

"I bring the intensity of my inner life, very personal emotions, into relation with these 'facts' of the world. I may be standing in the kitchen looking out of the window, or washing grains of rice for dinner. Or I may be folding a pile of laundry, yet within me there is an emotion that the gesture of my hands cannot reach.

"And often there is news of the world that reaches me. And I contemplate it. So really it is by looking long and hard, allowing the intensity of that otherness to enter in, that the charged rhythm of the poem, its music, comes. Breaks out onto the page."

I may not have said all this, there and then. And I wanted to speak of something that was too hard for me at the time: the migration of sense a poem requires, the way writing is tied up, for me, with loss, with what forces forgetfulness and yet at the very same time permits passage.

"A bridge that seizes crossing," I wrote in a poem, trying to touch the edge of migrancy that underwrites the sensible world for me. This was at a time when I felt that I needed to begin another life, to be born again. And now I think, for me, to be born again is to pass beyond the markings of race, the violations visited on us.

Awhile back there were a series of racial incidents in New York City. Two black children were spray-painted white, a white child raped in retaliation, an Indian child stoned. Haunted by these events, I made a poem called "Art of Pariahs." *Pariah* is a word that has come from my mother tongue, Malayalam, into English.

Perhaps one of the few benefits of colonialism is being able to infiltrate the language. I imagined Draupadi of the *Mahabharata* entering my kitchen in New York City. The longing to be freed of the limitations of skin color and race sing in the poem.

A year later I was in Delhi for an international symposium, put together by the Sahitya Akademi. Writers, artists, filmmakers were invited to ponder the ethnic violence that was threatening the fabric of secular India. Worn out by the flight that had got me in at one in the morning, I turned up a few minutes late for the start of the conference. The hall at the India International Center was packed. There were half a dozen people on the dais, dignitaries including Mulk Raj Anand, grand old man of Indian letters, the novelist who had written about the lives of Untouchables. There was no room in the auditorium, nowhere for me to sit. I stood uneasily at the edge, casting about for a place to sit, watching as a man dressed in white khadi, looking much as I would imagine a contemporary Tagore, spoke eloquently about the destruction of Babri Masjid and the communal riots in different parts of the country. "Our novelists will write about this," he said, "but it will take them several years to absorb these events." He paused, then added, "As the poet said." After what seemed like a space for a long, drawn-out breath, he recited the whole of "Art of Pariahs." He did not mention the poet's name, but anonymity made the matter more powerful as the poem, in his voice, flowed through the packed room. And listening, standing clutching my papers, I felt emotions course through me, deeper than the power of words to tell. For a brief while, a poem composed in solitude in a small New York City room had granted me the power to return home.

Art of Pariahs

Back against the kitchen stove
Draupadi sings:

In my head Beirut still burns.

The Queen of Nubia, of God's Upper Kingdom
the Rani of Jhansi, transfigured, raising her sword
are players too. They have entered with me
into North America and share these walls.

We make up an art of pariahs:

Two black children spray painted white
their eyes burning,
a white child raped in a car
for her pale skin's sake,
an Indian child stoned by a bus shelter,
they thought her white in twilight.

Someone is knocking and knocking
but Draupadi will not let him in.
She squats by the stove and sings:

The Rani shall not sheathe her sword
nor Nubia's queen restrain her elephants
till tongues of fire wrap a tender blue,
a second skin, a solace to our children

Come walk with me towards a broken wall
—Beirut still burns—carved into its face.
Outcastes all let's conjure honey scraped from stones,
an underground railroad stacked with rainbow skin,
Manhattan's mixed rivers rising.[2]

What might it mean for Manhattan's mixed rivers to rise?
How shall we move into a truly shared world, reimagine eth-
nicities, even as we acknowledge violent edges, harsh borders?
These children in Manhattan, the Muslim women raped in
Surat, the Hindu women stoned in Jersey City, coexist in time.
Cleft by space, they forge part of the fluid diasporic world in
which I must live and move and have my being.

I think of Derek Walcott's "terrible vowel, / that I!"[3] And I
understand that my need to enter richly into imagined worlds
cannot shake free of what my woman's body brings me. I cannot
escape my body and the multiple worlds of my experience.

And the sort of translation the poem requires—"translate"
in an early sense of the verb, meaning to carry over, to transport, for after all what is unspoken, even unspeakable must be
borne into language—forces a fresh icon of the body, compli-
cates the present until memory is written into the very texture
of the senses.

NOTES

1. Published in *Transformations* 9, no. 2 (Fall 1998), special issue on race and gender. Some portion of these reflections were presented at "Trade Routes: History, Geography and Culture: A Conference Towards the Definition of Culture in the Late Twentieth Century," Johannesburg, South Africa, October 15, 1977.

2. Meena Alexander, *River and Bridge.*

3. Derek Walcott, "Names," in *Collected Poems* (New York: Farrar, Straus and Giroux, 1986), 306.

Silenced Writer

Silenced writer. I start with that.

Without silence the words we treasure, the words we measure our lives by, could not appear.

But *silenced* is different.

I see a child who has no books, no pens, and scribbles words in the dirt, words that threaten to fly off and join the stick insects on the bark of a nearby tree. I see a grandmother dressed in a wrinkled white sari, her hand on the cloth that covers her thigh, over and over again she marks the jut and whorl of a classical script she has taught herself with difficulty.

She writes lines that can never appear, skid of invisible script. I see bodies in public places, bodies threatened, beaten, banned. Barbed wire, coils of it glinting in sunlight. Bars of a prison cage, the writer crouched inside, parrots above the cage chattering in heat. In the marketplace fear so palpable, people wrinkle up their noses and cover their faces with their handkerchiefs.

Fear stinks, no one can breathe properly.

Who will have the courage to write?

I see tunnels of smoke, gushing flame where once the great libraries stood. Barbarians, their faces covered with ski masks, looting, burning. Brick, mortar, marble melting, together with the precious imprints of hundreds and thousands of human souls. The barbarians are scared of these traces.

And the barbarians, who are they?

Where are they? Are they outside our gates? Or are they within?

NOTE

Published in *PEN America* (Spring 2004).

Words in the Wind

A cold day, the temperatures have dipped below normal. I see the black latticework of winter trees, glisten of light on the street. Lines come to mind, by the poet Huda Naamani who wrote in Beirut in a season of war:

> We will write our bodies with snow, the soul
> remains a horizon.

I imagine a woman in Baghdad. She waits for the bombs to fall. What is it like to live, waiting for bombs to fall?

She wakes in the morning light. She washes herself, combs her hair, touches her throat. She hears again the voice she heard in dreams. It is her own voice, torn from her body.

Here come back. It's not safe out there.

She is calling to her children—I gave birth to you and now you must come back.

But they do not hear her. When she wakes she sees the wall, the street. She learns to understand you can't turn time back.

I live far away from her, in the country that is sending thousands of young people to fight in Iraq. Other means of change are possible, and may well be within arm's reach. Why this massive military buildup? For oil? For a ghostly empire?

No blood for oil is the chant of thousands of antiwar demonstrators in cities across this country and all over the world. It is a cry that needs to be heard.

When fire rains down on the heads of innocent people, when soldiers start fighting and people start dying as they will, how shall we continue our ordinary lives?

What will become of our so-called normalcy?

How will we cross the street, bring our children home from school, approach our lovers, bury our dead?

Steel from the twin towers was melted down, used to make a battleship. Is this what the new world brings?

Rather than making the first war of a new century, we should make an effort to stitch together peace, a difficult and necessary peace. A harvest of light.

Somewhere on a city street a woman surrenders her scarfs.

They are black. The wind blows them back.

NOTE

Published on the Internet website Open Democracy, www.opendemocracy .net/conflict_iraq/article_882.jsp#14.

Mortal Tracks

In Rummana Hussain's work time brushes past, halt us in our tracks.

One side of the gallery space is swept by swaths of dark fabric tethered to embroidery rings, delicately notched with silver stitches.

Are these veils we touch, the woman's flesh curtained, her ghostly presence hinted at, the inside and outside of her life swept up in partitions, suspending time?

The monitor on the far wall, with its still image halts us. The blue and ochre colors of the hospital. The artist's arm with an IV dripping into the veins.

There is a mistiness to the image; then sharp clarity draws attention. Precisely the flesh that could not be seen, could only be hinted at by the suspended veils. And now in the place of healing, a hospital, a necessary invasion.

This is the same Rummana who made self-portraits for her show in Basel last year, two figures shown side by side, one of the artist swathed in a veil, the power of her two hands upholding a camera granting her visibility in world; and a companion image of the same figure, now with dark glasses, veil swept back, torso disrobed to reveal, through the blurred lens, the flattened scar of a mastectomy.

For this is a world in which the body of the artist, living and suffering, by embodying time quite simply produces the aesthetic space for us, a space in which we can see ourselves anew.

It is this power that we treasure, the fragile, mortal body, the "I" who enters into the world and then must vanish.

Somehow in facing this work (Rummana Hussain and I are practically the same age, both born in India in the aftermath of Partition) a line from John Donne's poem flashes up: a plea in the face of mortality: *not one hour I can myself sustain.* And yet of course it is precisely a self-sustaining that this art presents us with.

In her video *In Between* we see the figure of the artist, her form weakened by radiation treatment, walking precariously, in slow motion over the Queensborough bridge.

There is a resolute strength to her step, and we notice the stubborn curiosity that guides her. Her clothing is arresting. Simple black trousers and T-shirt fit for a Western metropolis, or indeed for life in Bombay, in some ways the most westernized of Indian cities, but on her feet are elaborate anklets knotted with a red cord, ghunghrus whose chiming sounds, reminiscent of the traditional dance forms of India, resonate with the flashing tassels braided into her hair, the hammered silver earrings that catch the light from the metal bridge.

Where is she going, we wonder, this figure dressed in her hybrid clothing?

What will she find as she crosses over?

As if to heighten the question of passage, the subway train curves over.

A metallic transport, bringing to mind the fractured time of migration. The present cut by memories of an elsewhere clarifies in the solarized shots of a train that has pulled into Bombay Central, people jostling, crowding in, a man his newspaper lifted over his face, as if to shield it.

Then we face the life of South Asian migrants in New York: a vendor of newspapers on the underground platform, moving figures in a shop stuffed with sweets and savories, lilt of saris and kurtas in a mirrored boutique, heavy flashing gold of a jewelry shop, polished purple of an eggplant, green karela, mint and coriander in a vegetable shop, a seller of after-dinner treats, paan and frozen kulfi, his little cart set out on the sidewalk.

And toward the end of the video, the interior of an apartment, the figure of a woman who before she stirs the food in her cooking pot chops carrots, peppers, onions at enormous speed—counterpoint to the slow motion of the figure on the bridge—and with the broken rhythm of her hands, revealing fragmented acts, continuous in their repetitive rhythm, a labor that recomposes memory, sustains life in a new world.

NOTE

Published in the catalog for the show "*Rummana Hussein* in Order to Join," *Art in General*, New York, October 1998.

Life Lines

The dividing lines of our lives, the broken borders of nations, enter powerfully into Zarina Hashmi's work. Migrancy itself becomes the ground of memory, an existential imperative that gathers together dispersed spaces. We see how borders that cut us apart can bind us together again.

In a series of six woodcuts called "Atlas of My World" Zarina reveals the stark lines of water and earth that mark the earthly spaces she has inhabited, in the course of her cosmopolitan life. But violence underwrites this mapping, first the violent Partition of the Indian subcontinent where she was born.

Locations become bruised abstractions, veering into beauty as the texture of the paper and black ink reveal a map that is shorn of the human beings who have torn and quartered it.

In *Dividing Line,* a woodcut of 2001, marks on paper create a glistening set of dark tracks that need no one, and that no one can be saved from.

For a portfolio of nine woodblock prints, using Urdu text, Zarina has picked a title, drawn from Adrienne Rich's translation of Ghalib, a circuitous flow of translated sense—"These Cities Blotted into the Wilderness." Here she maps out war zones, maps of ethnic conflict, burning buildings. The series begins with Grozny, blocks of dark color against a neutral background, moves onto Baghdad depicted with the flow of its curving river waters, then the city of Ahmedabad which stands out in shards, like a deftly broken mirror, and lastly New York, post-9/11, pictured in sheer black, with two lines of vertical light passing through.

As I reflect on her prints, I imagine a whole cycle of poems waiting to be written in response to her fierce and beautiful work.

These images are to be found in *Zarina: Weaving Memory* (Mumbai: Bodhi Arts, 2007). Also included in that catalog is my poem "House of Breath," dedicated to Zarina. The poem is printed in my book *Quickly Changing River* (Evanston, IL: TriQuarterly Books, Northwestern University Press, 2008).

This Is Not Me!

It was like this world's pleasure / and the way to the other / both walking towards me.

—Akkamahadevi (twelfth century)

Chila Kumari Burman and I live on two separate continents, she in London, I in Manhattan. Ghostly maps limit our lives, yet the unfurling of national borders, street signs, subway maps, none of this could make sense without the sharpness of locality, the dailiness of the living breathing world in which we find ourselves.

Through the mail Chila has sent me a large brown packet filled with images. They tumble out, sonorous colors, I see the brilliant red of two cups, the turquoise shimmer of another pair, then apsara women, flattened out, swimming, a density of desire that makes for an eternal present. These images will form part of the Hello Girls! exhibit in London.

I lay out the images on my dining table and keep sorting through them, looking at them, almost as if they were snapshots of a place I have not yet entered. Through the open window, for its summer time now, come the sounds of the New York City street, voices in English, Spanish, a child crying out after his ball, the seller of ice cream, candy floss. The trees are green, huge, almost as if midsummer were on us, and we, at the edge of an imaginary India.

There is a way in which the subcontinent underwrites us both. A subcontinent, colonized, torn apart by Partition, yet remaking itself and us so that memories and fantasies that pour through our skins, and some memories that we cannot even name, become, in their very exigency the route we must take to enter our own bodies.

When I speak about Partition to Chila, she, with ancestral memories of the Punjab, says to me:

"Yes, that's why my dad left, isn't it?"

And I nod, though of course the phone line only gives us murmurs, edits, vocal scrawls, and I force myself to lay out an unfinished thought and I blurt out:

"In the South we weren't really touched by Partition."

Yet of course that isn't quite true; in as much as India exists, the Partition made a very different kind of sense in the south of the country.

And Chila continues, in this back and forth: "and so I was born here."

Here for her, is Britain, and she is by rights a British artist, Black British in the complex minoritization of selves that allows us markers of belonging in these countries of the North where our bodies can never be taken for granted. Here for me is the United States, where I am Asian American, as a multiethnic taxonomy permits me. But Chila and I are both Indian women, and that allows for an immediacy of connection, a frisson of knowledge.

I think of Chila's *Portrait of My Mother,* the gentle, sad straightforward face of a young Indian woman facing the camera. What lies in the world beyond that seeing eye? The daughter reads the mother with all the tenderness incipient in the clarity of that first connection and then shows us the British pound note, mark of sovereignty, as light as lace, as fierce as a metallic brand, over that beloved face. Chila was born in England, and her parents raised her in Liverpool in a Punjabi-speaking home. Her mother must have regularly touched, folded those pound notes with the monarch's face on them.

My own mother raised in a nationalist family in India, refused to let her lips part when they had to sing "Rule Brittania" in college. She imparted to me her own proud, edgy animus toward the English language and then when I was six watched from a hazy distance as I was taught to curtsey to the Queen who was visiting the British school where I studied, in a small North African town on the banks of the Nile where we spent years of my childhood.

What does it mean to write over a mother's face, layer over a mother with the imprimatur of a colonial state? And of course part of the poignancy and indeed subtle tension of the image comes from the imagined maternal qualities of the royal face.

But to return to my question and try to respond. It is an act that the postcolonial daughter has to undertake, in her art, her writing. What other genealogy can we have, we who are cast outside the borders of the taken for granted? We whose bodies are scrawled over by the borders we have crossed?

There is an iconic quality to another face that Chila has printed over, her own image of 1992 intricately decked in traditional Indian jewelry, then spray-painted with the large gawky letters THIS IS NOT ME!

It's an image that haunts me. The gleam of dark eyes through vermillion spray paint, pallor of cheekbone, jut of jaw, the bodily self disowned. After all being female is not something added to race but comes fused with it, as part of my inalienable bodily being. Perhaps the most devastating effect of racism is to render one homeless in one's own body. So that as I walk the street or enter the building with great stone pillars, I absent myself from my body, become a fly in the blue air watching, seemingly free of threat.

Indeed the flip side, dark chromatic lining to the fly-in-the-air-scenario would be to walk down Main Street or enter that building intricately dressed in sari and blouse having scrawled on one's forehead and eyelids and cheeks, in crimson, the letters: THIS IS NOT ME! And such forcible, almost automatic absenting of "I" from my body is something that survivors of trauma understand, if only mutely, and something that racism in its multiple forms is able to enforce.

So that even as from inside ourselves, a voice comes, searching for sense, we must step out of our skins. They are written up, scrawled over, marked too much to be part of what we are. Yet we cannot live as skinless things. How shall we figure ourselves afresh, make up our lives in a diasporic world?

In Chila's work, I see her unique way of addressing this question, one possible aesthetic for a postcolonial theater of sense.

Think of the race thing, the body scrawled over. If we step back a little, we sense that it's all a bit of flimflam, this "race" thing, something baseless, ready to dissolve. After all, what could be more absurd?

And the self that is crossed out so painfully becomes flighty, multiple, caught in the shifting strands that make up the un-moored consciousness, delighted in its fortuitous nature, free. Now of course this transition is a provisional thing, but neces-sary counterpart to the torment of self, part of the shift to the swelling delight in the world of the senses.

Hence the transition we see in Chila's work from *This Is Not Me* to the sheer exuberance of the multiple figures of self-fashioning in *28 Positions in 34 Years* (1992), the daughter's face split into so many, gazing out at the world, a species of sorcery, fantastic play. Or in the richly textured, jewel-like surface of *Auto-Portrait, Fly Girl Series* (1993).

There too, is the element of riposte: You scrawled over me with your gaze, made me into a flat surface, so I shall take the power that is mine, become these shifting gorgeous surfaces, thrust the images back into your face. You can't touch me! You can't catch me!

Indeed the Don't Touch Me element is crucial here. The task of flight, necessary, seductive, a charged evasion of having been being rendered powerless. The power is in making images, im-ages of my own body, dark, female, which I can render on flat surfaces, deploy as I wish. To argue which is not to deny of course the coruscating surfaces of a postmodernist artifact, one that could only come into being in the late twentieth century.

When I communicate with Chila by fax about the provenance of Hello Girls! she says:

"I was running a workshop for Asian girls." This was during a residency in Glasgow. She asked the young women to bring in personal objects for use in their artwork, and she herself, in the evening turned to whatever personal items lay at hand:

"As I hadn't brought in many objects with me, or family snaps, I decided to use my clothes and whatever I had in my suit-case . . . I had bras with me, bikini, shalwar kameez and Indian shawls . . . so I started playing with the colors, changing the col-ors for the background and something was happening . . ."

"Why bras?" I ask her.

And Chila replies in terms of her characteristic concern with a visuality that exists in tension with the matter-of-fact reality of the world:

"I've always been interested in content and form," she tells

me, "so it's not just about a critique of the Wonderbra advert."
And she continues: "I was initially interested in abstracting the
BRA SHAPE so that you couldn't tell it was a bra, I was left with
color and form and the content. i.e. Bra wasn't easily visible,
because I'm very interested in color/form/abstraction i.e. I
wanted it to look flat from a distance . . . I'm not so much interested in the fact of representing a bra, its more the vulnera-
bility, the bra straps and shape has and the power of the bra
shape or form/object. Also bras are like EYES—eyes are crucial
in our culture."

Eyes, windows of the soul, site of desire, turned to the postcolonial riposte, a coruscating feminist tack, a sail on rough
waters. My mind moves to lines by Kamala Das I read as a
young poet, the exuberant travail of an Indian woman ac-
knowledging her own body, breasts, thighs, pubis all marked in
the coming to knowledge of what it might mean to refuse to be
a dark continent:

> I am today a creature turned inside
> Out. To spread myself across wide highways
> Of your thoughts, stranger, like a loud poster
> Was always my desire, but all I
> Do is lurk in shadows of cul de sacs,
> Just two eyes showing . . . oh never mind, I've
> Spent long years trying to locate my mind
> Beneath skin, beneath flesh and underneath
> The bone.[1]

What does it mean to search under the bone? It means to
touch the ghostly body, what one might even call the soul.

Indeed there is a ghostly emptiness in the bras, right through
the sheer sonorous delight of color. The images that bounce
off the walls, multiply in a dizzying phosphorescence, each de-
tail crystalline, marking out the boundaries of shifting scenes,
bodily unselvings.

Our conversation turns to bras, what it meant to learn to
wear them as girls, the discomfort of wearing ill-fitting bras, the
odd ways the points stuck out in wrongly shaped bras. "They are
always designed by men, aren't they," Chila muses. And I think

of when I returned to India in the early seventies after my student days in England, how a friend in the women's movement in India who had given up on bras, took to knotting her choli under her breasts in the way that peasant women did and encouraged me to do the same; and I think of Chila's vivid, phantasmagoria of bras against the backdrop of the Breast Cloth controversy in India, well before either of us was born, when the British colonial rulers found themselves taking sides in what was to become the Woman Question, ruling on whether lower-caste women had the right to wear bodices, cover their breasts.

I muse on the sheer delight of color in Chila's billboard-sized poster, the delicate textures we could bury our faces in, the twoness of the cups, echoing all the couplings that make for the bodily self, right breast and left breast, right hand and left hand, right thigh and left thigh, right eye and left eye, but also the *via negativa* of our social imaginaries, *neti-neti*, not this, not that, I am not this nor that, quintessential being, unnameable, a succor, a vanishing.

In our conversations Chila and I speak at length on how we were raised as Indian girls and subject of clothing.

When Chila says to me, "I wasn't even allowed to wear a skirt till I was sixteen," her words have an immediate resonance for me. I had to cover my arms and legs when visiting my father's village in a remote part of Kerala. Wear longer skirts in a Kerala town than I had to when visiting England. The constant taking off and putting on of garments, skirts, blouses, saris, cholis, kurtas, salwars, pants, coats and in the distance, bikinis, miniskirts, foisted on the bodily self a great fragility. Yet one that could lead to exuberant strategies, the casting off of one identity for another and yet another, fluid selves, porous boundaries.

After all to survive with one's integrity could oddly enough mean taking apart and putting together any possible self, given a present in which one was forced on stage with parts one had not picked to play, lines that crossed each other out, sighs, exhalations, coughs, grunts, sentences that refused translation, syntaxes that made for such a cacophonous crosshatch of memory, that merely to think them, would turn one into the equivalent of a loud poster. A blatant, burnished thing.

And under it, the tender soul, the "I," cryptic, illegible.

So by phone and by fax, Chila and I speak and write some more about the images in the show. We share thoughts, impressions. I muse on what a poet's version of a body print might be, the immediacy of language bordering on babble, the raw textures of touch.

There are body prints done when Chila was in India, during an international workshop in Modinagar near Delhi. I see the dark red color of breasts and belly raised and rimmed with the tiny bits of mica that decorate skirts, blouses, embroideries. Other body prints laid out in mandala style, the whole tracing a line of descent from work she started in the late seventies and eighties, *Body in Sugar* of 1978, mixed media on canvas, *My Breasts* of 1984 done with sugar and India ink monoprint or *Body Print* of 1987 with acrylic and glitter monoprint. The rotund anonymous shapes are essentially female, primitive, headless. There is no "I" there, only the flesh that makes up the subject.

Then there are figures of women some with heads draped, anonymous, nude, haunting figures each alone, against a wall. Naked women in blue. Blue figures against a blue wall. They are posing for the camera, for themselves turned camera. What are these postures that they take in this theater of sense, consciousness split into two, lighting up the melancholic body. Who are they these ghostly women, where do they come from? And what connection do they bear to the fragment of text from the Amar Chitra Katha comic entitled *Tales of Valiant Queens*? After all they reappear within those complex multicolored figurations. Are they split-off parts of the valiant queens, restless roaming others I need to acknowledge, selves unhoused?

The Amar Chitra Katha comics are familiar in the rooms of Indian children. A surefire way to learn of figures from history, the Rani of Jhansi set side by side with Draupadi, the literal past and the mythological past commingled as it enters into the child's imagination.

"Talk to me," I fax Chila, "about 'The Tales of the Valiant Queens.' I think of it as an Amar Chitra Katha comic. Often that's how children learn of the Rani of Jhansi and others. And these images become so crucial to us as we step out of our skins."

And Chila replies in the way of an artist, laying out the

palimpsest of self-fashioning. So that in a world without ready anchorage what one has made—and this is a process I see in my own responses—turns into the thread of sense, guiding one through the labyrinth of what has already been:

"I think we are all QUEENS because of how much we have survived and achieved, so I'm saying here are the Tales of Us Valiant Queens. I've done another piece in my monograph p. 57 called Dad on Ship Coming to England and like the three Queens which are the Queen of England I've deliberately put a wall over her face and the other Queen is my mum and the other my Grandmother!"

Chila goes onto speak of the erotic flow of sense between women, the way in which the swimming girls, apsaras blue as the water they swim in, become a trope of freedom. "I'm mad about these girls because they're active and gentle and blue," says Chila. "Also I go swimming nearly everyday and have done so for years, I used to swim in the school swimming club team."

In one of the images I see a girl, blue and active swimming away from a heavy seated figure, nude and masked, bound by gravity. Surely both figures are parts of a self, female, rendered fleshly. The heavy seated figure has a black cloth slipping off her shoulders, revealing her body. We witness a posture of power, yet there is something in there of the abject, a heavy body seated on the floor in a white room, not moving.

And in another frame, next to the sign TALES OF VALIANT QUEENS, there she is again masked and seated, in a realm of collage, a theater of bit and pieces, and others by her, one a dark nude body, female; the other her head covered, saturated in brilliant red and green. And Chila tells me that she wanted the masked nude figure "to look like a CHIEF . . . too weighted down with all the pressure of the world, but still very sharp and alert and content but vigilant."

Yet the counterpoint is insistent: there she is, a blue swimming girl, slipping out of the flounces, swimming away from the heavy seated figure with mask, the one who cannot move, who cannot show her face. And the other swims, swims away. Below her Lord Krishna, on an agarbati cover, plays his flute.

I think of how the swimming girls live in the fluidity of water. They can cross borders with the flick of an arm or thigh. Their breasts are uncovered. No Breast Cloth controversy has touched them, nor Victorian prudery.

While here we are with bras straps that hurt our bodies, writing, making images. And the bra stands in as simulacrum. The skins we slip from in order to be what we are. I muse on the double mimicry of a spotted bra (tiger skin markings) against paisley. "OOO pure designs that have us," I write to Chila.

And when she writes back she tells me that the tiger bra is really a bikini top and that the Hello Girls piece will be very big ten meters by four meters THIS SHAPE and she encloses the words in a rectangle so I can see what the shape will be.

For me the art of Chila Kumari Burman is about the freedom of the subject, the rights of the female body, intricate self-fashioning. We see this all the way from her overtly political mural work, *Southall Black Resistance Mural* of 1986 done in collaboration with Keith Piper, through the *Shotokan* images of 1993, her own body, sari clad, superb, trained in the martial arts, filled with motion, resistant.

Can the notion of *corps vécu,* body embedded in the flesh of the world that Merleau-Ponty outlined, work for us? It is a notion I first came across as a young university student in England, sifting through phenomenology to find a way in which my history as a young woman from India and Africa could be real for me. Can we race the *corps vécu* all the way to the edge of the twenty-first century? Can it be useful to us, women artists of the South Asian diaspora? A dark *corps vécu,* I think, with stretch marks . . . And why not? After all what could make more sense when one is searching out rites of passage for the soul cupped to a body, forced to search out pathways through skin and bone?

NOTES

Published in *n.paradoxa,* issue 14, 2001.

1. Kamala Das, "Loud Posters," in *The Old Playhouse and Other Poems* (New Delhi: Orient Longman, 1973), 47.

III. Migrant Memory

Questions of Home

People sometimes ask me, "Did you always want to be a poet? Is that what you really wanted?" I reply as truthfully as I can. First of all I wanted to be circus performer—not just any performer but a tightrope artiste. I knew the word *artiste* and felt it was very grand, and that was precisely what I wanted to be. My grandfather had taken me to see the Gemini Circus in Kerala when I was six. I was so struck by the skinny girls in their tinsel costumes, amazed at their balancing feats. Neither the fact that they were obviously shivering on the ground in their skimpy outfits—for it was monsoon time and chilly—nor the fact that I had no head at all for heights, deterred me from what I longed for.

Back home, I tried to balance on the bamboo pole that someone had forgotten and left behind—it ran between the rabbit hutch and the hen house, both low concrete structures. I fell off, skinned my knees. Grown nervous at the wobbly pole, and my inability to walk a straight line, I tried to practice on the sandy courtyard.

With a twig I drew lines in the sand and tried to walk along. I shut my eyes, feeling that was the best way to get a feel for heights and understand, with some measure of safety, the dizziness that comes with impossible balancing acts. I understood very quickly what I still know—whether in life or in art, it is very hard for me to walk an utterly straight line.

My next thought of how to live was an ambition that was instilled in me by my grandfather and aided and abetted by my mother—I should be a medical doctor, I was told, and do some good in the world. After all, India needed doctors. Which country needs poets? My father kept himself clear of this particular discussion. He was a scientist and had studied physics at university before turning to meteorology and he felt that the methods of scientific inquiry were the closest we could come, through our conscious minds, to truth. Might the study of physics be the way forward, for me, as well? But I was lousy at math and found the computations of physics impossible, and as for chemistry, what I loved best were the colors in the test tubes. I kept staring at the bubbling multicolored liquids rather than at the hypotheses I was supposed to deal with.

Then poetry happened. That is the only way I can put. I started writing poetry young, when I was eleven or twelve. The reason why I keep writing is still the same. For me, it is the music of survival. There is an inner voice that speaks to me, makes music out of words, makes notes out of syllables, makes rhythms out of what words cannot reach.

Each year of my life, from the age of five to the age of eighteen, I traveled across continents, from India to Sudan and back again. Sometimes the journey back involved a detour to Europe, or to Egypt or Lebanon. At the Bandung Conference Nehru, the prime minister of India, had met Azhari, the president of Sudan, and it was decided between them that technical assistance would be sent from India to the newly independent African country. Doctors, lawyers, judges, scientists, teachers— all traveled across the Indian Ocean. My father, a young man at that time, and working as a meteorologist for the government of India, decided to try his luck. He was "seconded abroad," as the phrase had it, to work in that other country.

I wonder what it was that made my father want to move for a few years. Perhaps that spirit of adventure that never left him, a need to see glimpse another horizon, with all its attendant difficulties. With his decision my young life was altered forever. I turned five on the steamer as my mother and I traveled from Bombay to Port Sudan, to meet him. I still think that birthday on the deep waters of the Indian Ocean has marked me in ways utterly beyond my ken. And it has left me with the sense that home is always a little bit beyond the realm of the possible, that a real place in which to be, though continually longed for, can never be reached and stands brightly lit at the edge of vanishing. I think of Mallarmé who evoked the image of *l'absente de tous bouquets*—the quintessential flower absent from all bouquets.

For me, that is what home is. And our migrations become the music, wave after wave of it, that gives it a fragile and precarious shape.

Can one find a home in language? I feel so. At least, that is what I have tried to do. I left India too young to attain literacy in my mother tongue, Malayalam, a great Dravidian language with proud traditions of literary culture. I speak it fluently and the rise and pour of that language has shaped the kind of poet I am. I had Hindi as a child, and as I grew older English took its place in my mind, and became for me a language of crossing and of delivery.

The English I use bends and flows to many other languages. For me it is the language of Donne and Wordsworth as well as a postcolonial tongue and it exerts an intimate violence, even as I use it, make it mine. Yet surely each language, each script, exerts its pressure. It seems to me that a poet works with words as a painter works with color—as matter she cannot do without, living material into which she must translate what would otherwise remain inchoate.

My earliest poems, which I wrote at the ages of ten and eleven, were composed in French. It seemed to me having been made to learn a few lines by Verlaine, by heart in school—I refer to Unity High School in Khartoum, Sudan—that French was surely the only language fit for the lyric. Mercifully none of my earliest French poems survived. Soon enough my affections shifted and I found in English a more capacious instrument for my longing. But those earliest longings, as they found expression in poetry, were flattened out, imitations of Toru Dutt and Sarojini Naidu, cut and pasted as it were, onto white paper. Indeed I found in those early Indian women composers of poetry in English something of the circuitry of sense that a colonial childhood had instilled in me. And there was Verlaine whose subdued, yet febrile lines, spoke very directly to me. And Rabindranath Tagore, whose poems in English translation from *Gitanjali, The Gardener,* and *Fireflies.* But it was his play *The Post Office,* telling as it did of the death of a young boy, that haunted me, and indeed haunts me still. Someday I said to myself I will make a poem and evoke the way in which as children in India, my cousins and I, put on the play for our immediate family. A Bengali play, translated into English and acted out in the courtyard of a Kerala house, in the constant presence of Malayalam, our mother tongue. Yet we spoke the words in Tagore's own English translation, in our lisping Indian English.

In the Sudan where I spent a good part of each year, in the north of the country, the language was Arabic. As a teenager I had a group of poet friends who wrote in Arabic and it was my friends who translated a few of my English poems and submitted them to the local newspaper. My very first publications were in Arabic, the language of the place in which I lived, but a language which I could not read or write, though I could indeed speak it with a certain fluency. People would come up to me and say, "I saw your poem in the newspaper." And then add, something like "I really liked it" or "I didn't really get it. What was it about?" And all I could do was shake my head and smile wistfully, making it clear that while I read and wrote English, I could not lay claim to the same talent in Arabic. So it was that my life as a poet began in translation, that connection to a reading public which alone could allow me a "real" existence. So it was that a translated life held sway.

As a girl child I wrote in secret, in the bathroom so no one would see. I hid my scribblings in the folds of my knickers. I felt a sense of shame at what was so intimate to me, felt that what I had made could never measure up to what the world believed in. So in some sort of panic I set up the world and its measurements as forever inimical to what I might write. At the very same time I held onto the belief that the things I made were fierce and pure and needed to exist. For I thought and still think of my poems as made objects.

It seems to me as I think back that right at the start I did not feel the need to share what I had written with others. It was enough that I had written the poem, that the poem existed. The need to share, to publish, to have others acknowledge what I had written, that desire, that longing came later. And perhaps that longing is also part of needing to belong, needing to be in place.

The composition of poetry cannot be cleft from the density of place, and the sights and sounds and smells the sensorium of the body makes us heir to. For place bears the mark of history. It is the wound that memory returns us to so that in poetry we can commemorate, we can remember. This elegiac function of poetry is of great importance, part of its ability to store the voices that otherwise would vanish. No I am not confusing the poem with what we think of as oral history, rather that within the poem the shadows cleft from their bodies, the rack, the wound, the violation all still live.

Poetry and place are bound up together. If poetry is the music of survival, place is the instrument on which that music is played, the gourd, the strings, the fret. I had sensed the truth of this, but certain difficulties befell me. To be a real writer—and I underlined the word *real* in red ink, in my own head—it seemed to me that I had to have grown up in one place, "one dear perpetual place." Even if I did not have Yeats's poignant phrase in mind, I did have a vivid sense that each great writer I knew had a language and a place to which he or she was wedded. And the language bubbled out of place as water from underground streams the earth concealed. In this way, it was an outcrop of the region, *desha-bhasha*.

There was Kumaran Asan, who lived in Kerala and wrote in Malayalam; Tagore, who lived in Santiniketan and wrote in Bengali; Verlaine, who lived in France and wrote in French; Shakespeare, who wrote in English and lived somewhere in England, that tiny island floating on a map that I had seen several times in school but could never quite make head or tail of. Lacking just one single place to call my home and shorn of a single language I could take to be mine and mine alone, I felt stranded in the multiplicity that marked my life and its rich coruscating depths drew me, or so I felt, into grave danger.

It took me quite a while to realize that I did not have to feel strung out and lost in the swarm of syllables. Rather, the hive of language could allow me to make a strange and sweet honey, the pickings of dislocation. I also understood dimly that I was not alone in this predicament and that I could gain a great freedom and indeed find sustenance for my art by flowing as well as

I could into the sea of migrant memory. Now I realize that writing makes an unquiet border to what I cannot ever fully put words to, nor ever completely leave behind.

A few years ago the poet Allen Ginsberg passed away. The week that he lay dying I read his *Indian Journals* with great care. I was struck by the clarity of place in his writing even as the Rajasthan of his imagination splintered into brilliant surreal fragments. Each day I took the book with me on the subway and getting off at Columbus Circle I pulled it out of my bag as I walked the few blocks uptown, by Central Park. Once or twice on my way to catch the cross town bus at Sixty-fifth, I sat on my favorite rock in the park, close to the street. I spread out my things, book bag, pen, paper, water bottle, and I read his journals again. I was near the park when I got news of Ginsberg's death.

I shut my eyes. I saw him in Rajasthan. He was walking with Mirabai in the heat. It was Rajasthan and it was not, it was Central Park and it was not. I saw Mira approach him by the black rock. Together they walked toward the lake.

I like my favorite people to meet, even if they are separated by thousands of miles and several centuries. So it was with these two poets. In "Indian April," an elegy for Ginsberg, I draw them together in the shining space of the imaginary—Mirabai and Allen Ginsberg and then, in the great silence of the invisible world, I hear them talk to each other.

NOTE

An earlier version of this essay was first published on the website of the Academy of American Poets, www.poets.org/malex.

The poem "Indian April" was published in my book *Illiterate Heart* (Evanston, IL: TriQuarterly Books, Northwestern University Press, 2002).

Obstinate Questionings

I propped open the dictionary—an old, fat one, immensely heavy—on the kitchen table. I have to use the magnifying glass to peer at the letters, tiny black letters dancing on the page. They might be a flurry of gnats on a summer's day.

But it's almost the end of winter and the trees are bare. There is a light sprinkling of snow on the river, and across the river's quiet depth are the rocks of New Jersey, an outcrop of granite, black obsidian, and gray-green gneiss.

How far away are those rocks? Perhaps a whole mile away? More? In any case, what would a mile mean? I can see those rocks, hold them in the mind's eye, and that is what matters.

In the kitchen I bend over the old, heavy dictionary, trying to figure out the meaning of the word I am in search of: *Dislocation.*

When I was a child in my grandmother Mariamma's house, a four-hundred-year-old house in Kozhencheri, on the west coast of Kerala, we had no electricity and I had to squint hard in the glow of the oil lamps to try and see the page of the book she would hold open on her knee. I would try to follow the letters as she moved her finger along the lines, parting and closing her lips, so slowly, as she read. Though my great-grandfather had been a philosopher, he had, in accordance with tradition, neglected the literacy of his daughters, and my grandmother Mariamma had come to reading a little late in her life and with some difficulty. Then, too, she was often tired when the day's work was over and she settled down by the porcelain lamp with its low fluttering wick. And those oil lamps, with their luminous, diffuse glow, did not ease the task of close reading.

Ten thousand miles away and three decades after my grandmother's death, in a house not by the Pamba River as hers was, but here, close to the river Hudson, I bend closer to the battered

Oxford English Dictionary, again trying to make out the words in front of me.

dislocation: to put out of place
locare: to place. Locus, place

Then follow other meanings, thick and fast. One I fasten onto: *to put out of place; to shift out of proper or former place; to displace.* Yet another that is striking to me: *to put out of proper position in relation to contiguous parts (without removal to a distance); also to displace (a bone) from its proper joint.*

I step back, close up the book and shut my eyes. Almost as if my consciousness were a discrete hollow, bits and pieces of places pour into me: the edge of a muddy stream, green leaves of a tree (I can smell the bitter bark), stones at the edge of a dry road, a wall white with sunshine, wings of a dove, somewhere over a slate-gray roof.

Images all, suspended in memory, yet bound to my sensual body. Except in my memory they could not exist and now that they are part of my mnemonic world, I have to make space for them.

I have to fabricate place so that these images can exist, not as mere bits and pieces of temporality, echoing in my inwardness, but as portions of a shining symbolic space, their fluttering parts redisposed in a poem.

When I say poem, I evoke what Wallace Stevens calls "the poem of the mind"—the fraught yet fluid meaning-making that allows us to be in the world. But what is also crucial is the labor peculiar to the poet, the material processes of writing and revising so that words stitch their way through the page, the humming hive of the brain and the multitudinous letters of the chosen alphabet bound each to the other in coruscating harmony.[1] This is the harmony that underwrites a poetics of dislocation, where multiple places are jointed together, and the whole is lit by desire that recuperates the past, figures forth the future, thread of gold at the rim of a black horizon.

At the edge of a new century, with its massive migrations of peoples, ceaseless circulation of goods and knowledge, cities that multiply their inhabitants, glittering websites and cyber knowledges, we need to think space: think space, through our blood and bones; figure out how space allows us to be, permits language, encodes, the poem. By which I mean that it grants the poem a *cadre intérieur,* a phrase I borrow from the Cubists, an inner frame, an internal index of sense.[2] And *sense,* here, I mean not as abstraction or aftermath, but rather a blossoming of words, out of flesh. *Vak* in the Sanskrit rendering of Word, Logos, what I imagine in an originary, most materialist sense that lets us come close to the rock's edge, an outcrop of black granite by the riverbank where many hands find hold.

In a poem called "San Andreas Fault" I face my muse: a creature dressed in a silk sari, gumboots on her feet; her body utterly weightless, she clings to rock. For me, the weightless body clinging to rock becomes an icon of nonplace, the zone the muse makes as she faces me. From her hold on black rock, she asks me questions, some so tormenting that I am forced to write a poem.[3] Those rocks came to me from the Pacific Coast, where I used to go to visit a dear friend. Now the rocks I see out of my window are part of the Palisades in New Jersey, across the river from where I live. I can see them when I step out of my apartment and walk out into the park. Time and again, the discrete portions of geography allow me to anchor my inner world, make a palimpsest of place. Without this rich and jagged density, landscapes real and imagined that layer over each other in time present, I could not make my poems.

As a small child, how did I attach myself to place? I shut my eyes and see a child in a tree. A girl child of four who has climbed up the smooth bark of a love apple tree. She is in a house of dark green leaves and will not come down. She hangs upside down by the crook of her knees and opens her eyes wide. Her white cotton skirt is bunched up between her small knees so it doesn't flap over her face. Her face is free for the light to shine on it— a face framed by leaves, but with the sky and leaves and earth visible to her. Neither leaves nor cotton skirt pounced upon by the wind can cover up her eyes or ears or nose.

She hangs there, gently rocking back and forth as the visible world flows through blades of grass in the garden, the warm bunches of mango on the mango tree, the circling sky lit by late monsoon clouds.

In lines of a poem called "Black River, Walled Garden," alluding to that time of childhood, I have written:

> I swayed in a cradle hung in a tree
> and all of the visible world—
> walled garden,
> black river—flowed in me.[4]

But perhaps "flowed through me" would express it better— the body of the child at the heart of the world of rock and stone and tree, the elements she mingles with, making her child's self portion of creation, clot of blood in a green tree.

It is where I began as a poet, and it has taken me all these years to find this place: a girl child hidden in a green tree, a safe and secret place.

There is no map that can coax her back into a world of crossed paths, circling aerial routes, rough sea voyages, all the morass of intercontinental crossings her parents enforce. She stays up in the tree and allows the fractured world to enter her, fluid as dream. This becomes the realm of metempsychosis, of deep migrancy.

There is a zone of radical illiteracy, a space that stands under both our hold of place and of syntax, a zone where I need to touch in order to make poems. And now I see that the child in the tree renders back what the woman in her search of a *via negativa* of meaning-making had lost, the glimmer of deep green leaves, the scent of ripe fruit, the whispering of many mouths in that first tree of life, child's flesh lit by sun and wind, earthly solace, surpassing words.

At eighteen I went to university in England to work on my Ph.D., and after a whole year of partying, strobe lights, harsh music, I settled down to reading and writing. Looking back, it seems to me that during those years of study I endured a constant low-grade fever, at least that is how it feels to me. I fastened on the poetry of William Wordsworth, questions of childhood and memory. But as the work grew I brought in several other poets, both

Romantic and Modern, and philosophers, too: Husserl, Sartre, and Merleau-Ponty, for I was trying to make up a theory of how consciousness etched out the poem, and how that etching was necessarily bound to sensuous space around the living body. I wanted to figure out how the poem, in its own way, doubles up as place, and grants the powers of self-fashioning to a consciousness dislocated by the inexorable passage of time. Cut away from the sensuous hold of place, the shards of memory would begin a slow, corrosive dissolution. I kept reading Merleau-Ponty's insight about bodily being, as if it might help me unlock some truth about the composition of poetry, or indeed about myself: "Our own body is in the world as the heart is in the organism: it keeps the visible spectacle constantly alive, it breathes life into it and sustains it inwardly, and with it forms a system."[5] Could the poem be read as a "system" etched into being by a unique body?

The poet I turned to again and again was Wordsworth. I gave my heart to him, a poet who tells of spaces shorn of words and hidden, torn nesting spots for a child who must wander out alone. And I can say this now, without embarrassment or irony, realizing how my late teenage focus on the poet of Cumbria, the site in 2001, of a slaughter of animals, for fear of a plague of almost biblical proportions, how that focus kept me from examining the world that I came from, a postcolonial world of great turbulence and self-questioning.

Yet in reading Wordsworth, a wound quickened for me—a wound that was not mine, yet carried resonances, as if from afar. Again and again I read to myself lines from the "Ode: Intimations of Immortality from Recollections of Early Childhood":

> But there's a Tree, of many, one
> A single Field which I have looked upon,
> Both of them speak of something that is gone[6]

In reading those lines, we glimpse the details of desire. It is this particular tree and no other; this single field that I have known and loved, light flashing on the soil, bent grass, tiny runnels of water. And perhaps, in turning to the Wordsworthian tree, I was able to forget the tree of my earliest years, and the child who hung there, clot of blood in a bushel of green leaves, fearful to descend. Or perhaps I was able to glimpse through his words that very tree I could not speak of, glimpse a consciousness that courses toward the darkest refinements of our knowledge—the groping, pulsing edges of what is given, an irreducible awareness of being human in a world that is neither all solid nor all there. How I treasured his words:

> . . . obstinate questionings
> Of sense and outward things,
> Fallings from us, vanishings

In a draft for my poem "Illiterate Heart," I used those lines as an epigraph, then cut them out, feeling the burden of the colonial past overmuch. But Wordsworth comes in as a ghostly figure whose hand passes through me. The intimate violence that I had absorbed with the language I used for my poems melding with my early fears about what it meant for me, an Indian woman, to write poetry. I imagine two male figures approaching me. The first is an important male poet in Malayalam, my mother tongue. And after him comes Wordsworth.

> So it was I began, unsure of the words
> I was to use still waiting for a ghost
> to stop me crying out:
> You think you write poetry! Hey you—
>
> as he sidestepped me dressed neatly
> in his kurta and dhoti,
> a mahakavi from the temples of
> right thought.
>
> Or one in white flannels
> unerringly English, lured from Dove Cottage,
> transfixed by carousels of blood,
> Danton's daring, stumbling over stones
> never noticing his outstretched
> hand passed through me.

What does it mean to be a poet whose flesh is marked in this way, with invisible hands passing through?

I have no real answer except to think that the living body is marked exquisitely, brutally, by what we call history, the history of culture, of many cultures. And that to survive we need to make sense of dislocation, flesh and bones and skin pulled out of joint.

That brings me to speaking of a tree; not the one in Wordsworth's reckoning, but its dark Other. Stouter, bloodier, it appears more than a century later at the heart of a geography of enforced migration, in a plot of torn territory. I see its trunk and leaves dappled by the shadow of its ghostly double, that "tree, of many, one" that Wordsworth touched, one and the other sedimented in time's transparencies.

I speak of the haunting fable "Toba Tek Singh," by the great short-story writer of Partition, Sadat Hasan Manto. The story is set in a lunatic asylum at the time of Partition.

When asked if he will go to India or to Pakistan—for in Manto's fabricated world, the inmates of the madhouse are given such a choice—one man clearly understands that neither country will do. Very simply, he says, "I wish to live in this tree."[7] He picks a single tree and installs himself there, his limbs dangling, sensing in that green cage the only safety he will ever find. Then there is that other mad creature at the end of the tale, too old to climb a tree, the one who speaks in the babble that no one can follow. He stands stock still on his swollen legs, refusing to move, till until he falls, flesh upon dirt, marking an untouchable zone, a no-man's-land.

Through these figures—each intensely human, each clinging to a spot of time, a morsel of space, this and no other—the ferocious logic of nation building is exposed, and we confront what Giorgio Agamben has called *la nuda vita,* naked or bare life.[8]

What kind of community is possible? In the furious process of national translation, who will survive? How will we find ourselves?

The pain of recognition emerges with numbing clarity in another short story by Sadat Hasan Manto. This, too, is set during the Partition of India. As so often in Manto's work, the body of woman becomes the site for the crosshatch of desire and violation.

An old man keeps searching for his lost daughter, who was torn from him in the tumult of refugee camps. All he has of her is her dupatta, which he had stuffed into his pocket. Hoping against hope that she has not been raped or killed, he sends young men out in search of his beautiful Sakina. At the very end of this tiny tale, all of three pages long, the father stands in a room in the local hospital. He sees the young woman with the mole on her cheek lying on a soiled stretcher and cries out her name. The doctor, trembling, turns to the father and asks him to open the window.

"Open the window" he says. They need air.

Hearing the words "open"—*khol do*—"open" in Urdu—the young woman stirs, gropes painfully for the cord that ties her shalwar at her waist, unties the shalwar, and opens her legs. The young doctor breaks into a cold sweat.[9]

If we meditate on the title of the English translation, "The Return," which is quite different from the Urdu "Khol Do," so terse and apt, one might ask who is returning, or what is being returned. The face of the teenager, she who is lovely and has a mole on the left cheek, a vivid mark beseeching recognition, draws the father back. But the young woman is utterly changed. The repeated rapes she has suffered have marked her psychic body with an invisible inscription that the command she hears forces into legibility. After such knowledge, what forgiveness? Yet Manto forces us to realize that it is precisely out of the moments of traumatic recognition, flashpoints of pain, that healing might come. And through such recognition language is split open, into a vividness that in its extreme, creative fragility, attaches to a new sense of place, to the multitudinous, teeming forms of life that we cherish.

NOTES

Published in *Haritham* 14 (Winter 2002).

Some of these reflections first emerged during my keynote presentation for the conference "Remapping the Modern: Cultural and Aesthetic Transformation in Asia," Rutgers University, March 29, 2001.

1. Wallace Stevens, "Of Modern Poetry," in *Collected Poetry and Prose* (New York: Library of America, 1997), 218. Consider also what Wordsworth calls "the picture of the mind" in "Lines Composed a Few Miles

Above Tintern Abbey"; see William Wordsworth, *Poems,* ed. Stephen Gill (New York: Oxford University Press, 1984), 133.

2. On the internal irruption of fragments into the art space, "L'objet reel . . . le cadre intérieur du tableau," see Guillaume Apollinaire, *Meditations Aesthetiques: Les Peintres Cubistes* (Paris: Hermann, 1965), 65.

3. Meena Alexander, *The Shock of Arrival: Reflections on Postcolonial Experience* (Boston: South End Press, 1996), 146.

4. Meena Alexander, "Black River, Walled Garden," in *Illiterate Heart* (Evanston, IL: TriQuarterly Books, Northwestern University Press, 2002).

5. Maurice Merleau-Ponty, *Phenomenology of Perception,* trans. Colin Smith (London: Routledge and Kegan Paul, 1970), 203.

6. William Wordsworth, "Ode: Intimations of Immortality from Recollections of Early Childhood," in *Poems,* 298, 301.

7. Sadat Hasan Manto, *Kingdom's End and Other Stories,* trans. Khalid Hasan (New Delhi: Penguin, 1989), 13.

8. Giorgio Agamben, *Homo Sacer,* trans. Daniel Heller-Roazen (Palo Alto, CA: Stanford University Press, 1988).

9. Manto, *Kingdom's End,* 38.

Facing Wordsworth

Confronting Wordsworth's poetry I have to admit to a pained love that is not easy to speak of, an attachment so deep that I have sometimes felt it would be easier to deny it. Like many children in a world marked by colonialism I had to learn his poem "I wandered lonely as a cloud" by heart. When I first visited England and saw daffodils growing in a field near the university where I was studying, they seemed so ordinary, and yet curiously unreal. It was the earlier brilliant flashing the poet had evoked that stayed with me. The flesh of those flowers is something I cannot free myself from. He evoked it in a language that was not mine, yet one that I have made my own, tugging and tearing at its skin so that it might accommodate the whisperings of my own heart.

I tried to imagine the pallor of the poet who penned the lines I loved, the clothes he wore, the winter cold he must have endured. Through Wordsworth I first realized that poetry could be powerfully autobiographical, that the materials of an ordinary life might be fit subject matter. I discovered that Wordsworth's poetry cut straight to the heart of my childhood, the hurt, the harm, the blessing. I kept thinking about the interior life the child bears within, so often cut away from the realm of words.

A few years ago, having read a poem by the Japanese poet Kasuya Eiichi called "Daffodils" I decided to compose my own poem with that very title. Running through my mind at that time were Wordsworth's blossoms, sighted near Derwent Water, golden petaled things that had flashed in on the poet's mind when he was aware only of his own drifting self-consciousness.

Elsewhere, Wordsworth's poetry bears witness to a self that is torn in two, yet healed in some measure through the use of the imagination, through the slow meditative power of words. I think of lines from Book 2 of *The Prelude:*

> . . . so wide appears
> The vacancy between me and those days
> Which yet have such self-presence in my mind
> That sometimes when I think of them I seem
> Two consciousnesses—conscious of myself
> And of some other Being.

We see clearly the task of memory, the difficult necessity of return to a past which can sometimes overwhelm the self, so that the present is thrust further away, further apart from that other time which holds emotional sway. Who or what is the self? The question haunts the poet of Grasmere.

I love the architecture of Wordsworth's thought, the relentless process of making meaning, the stops, the sift, the failing sense all part of it. I seem to hear him speak out loud as he broods on "the dark / inscrutable workmanship that reconciles / discordant elements, makes them cling together / in one society."

Yet it became clear to me, perhaps even right from the start though I could not bear to admit it then, that the slow, exclusionary power of his gifts, drew strength from what he thought of as a cherished, domestic landscape, the valley of Grasmere, a landscape which I as a woman, and a woman of color at that, could never enter with unquestioned ease. Wordsworth himself did not enjoy difference, and any otherness that crossed the borders of his valley seemed troublesome to him. After the early years of his revolutionary fervor there was a settling into a narrower sense of self, a growing conservatism. Yet the task of memory that Wordsworth sets up for himself, the careful sorting out of sense, the poring over the processes of thought, the necessity of return, stayed with me. I had lived through multiple migrations, across several continents, and his Grasmere was a dream, a dream of an unsullied green.

When I visited Dove Cottage I was struck by how securely Wordsworth's lines seem embedded in place, the outer rim of place making a horizon for the increasing difficulty of his thought, its metaphysical edge casting into relief the nothingness that underlies all qualities. The following lines convey the austerity, the musical gravity of his reckoning, a difficult world that poetry might take for its home:

> . . . forthwith I left the spot
> And reascending the bare Common saw
> A naked pool that lay beneath the hills
> The Beacon on the summit, and more near,
> A Girl who bore a pitcher on her head
> And seemed with difficult steps to force her way
> Against the blowing wind. It was in truth,
> An ordinary sight; but I should need
> Colours and words that are unknown to man
> To paint the visionary dreariness . . .

NOTE

Presented at the "Presiding Spirits" breakfast, Poetry International, Royal Festival Hall, London, October 27, 2002.

Composition

The here and now was never something I could take for granted. To be somewhere, was also to not be somewhere else. I now think that each rock, each root, even in the garden of my earliest childhood, carried its own shadow. In the poem, the visible and the invisible are entwined and place becomes a living palimpsest. The zone of the poem is where dreams cross language. And with the rhythms of composition the invisible enters.

In my early twenties, living in Hyderabad, I rented a room in an old house that had a magnificent courtyard set with tiles and potted vines with tumbling, fragrant jasmine. My room was on the far side of the courtyard from the main dwelling. One of my windows looked out onto the courtyard with its ancient tulasi plant set in a pedestal. The other window looked out onto a broken Muslim graveyard with its dry neem trees. In between tombstones wild goats grazed. Both house and graveyard were at the edge of Abid road. Where that road crossed another, often there was trouble.

The gate of the house was guarded by a great peepul tree. When it rained the leaves turned a dark green, the color of seawater when the sun vanishes. I wrote a poem called "Stone Roots."

At the time all I had published were three slim books from two small presses in Calcutta. I had a longing to write better, to make a lyric that would shine with the truth of the heart. The story of Yang Chu, a Chinese sage who knelt and wept at the crossroads, haunted me. By the time the book with the poem in it was published, I was in America. Words like *globalization* meant nothing to me. From time to time in my new country I read the poem. It reminded me of something I was trying to understand.

Stone Roots

I am afraid to go out
into the streets of Nampally,
the peepul trees drip.

Yang Chu wept at the cross
roads, each chosen road
divided the stone roots.

Trees understand the under
water base of stone,
the gravity of exile.

(Note: Yang Chu c. 350 B.C.
Legend has it he knelt and
wept at each cross-road
believing that any road
taken would lead to another
that crossed a neighboring
road, endlessly multiplying
the chances of being lost.)[1]

Slowly it came to me, with the psychic work of migration, the need to become American, to take citizenship. I had come from one democracy and wanted to be fully part of another. I wanted to be able to vote. I tried out figure out what it meant, that curious word *naturalization*—as if something in my very being were going to be altered. I was anxious, fearing I would be plunged into a new, unknown life. From time to time I walked down to the river Hudson and stared across the river at the cliffs of New Jersey.

The need to be born again, a fierce need to reinvent the self, is what drew me to America. For me that is the promise of this country, a promise, crossed with blood.

I stood in Riverside Park just as the leaves were starting to change color, a fragrance of gold in the air. There was an oil tank on the other side of the river with the word HESS written on it. I did not know what that word meant. Later someone told me that it was the name of a petroleum company. I wrote a poem called "River and Bridge."

Now when I think back to that moment and my solitude,

there at the crossroads, lines of a poem by Stephen Crane come to me—"Because it is bitter / And because it is my heart."

How to make sense of the heart? The classical worlds of East and West coexist for me in imagination, together with the scent of earth, from a childhood garden, which I carry always within. At the edge of winter, I capture that scent, watching an autumn leaf, a damp gold leaf blown down to ground.

Once again it was early November. Another war was at hand, the stock market had crashed. I waited with my family, in a crowded school cafeteria. As the long lines crept forward, there was a palpable tension in the air, a nervous excitement in all the people gathered there, a feeling that this time our votes could really count, that we had the power, if we dared to use it, to turn back the dark tide.

As we walked out, in fitful sunlight, the leaves on the trees by the river were blazing.

River and Bridge

Trees on the other side of the river
so blue, discarding light into water, a flat
white oil tank with HESS in black, a bridge
Holzer might skim with lights—I will take her
down before she feels the fear—no sarcophagus here:

I have come to the Hudson's edge to begin my life
to be born again, to seep as water might
in a landscape of mist, burnished trees,
a bridge that seizes crossing.

But Homer knew it and Vyasa too, black river
and bridge summon those whose stinging eyes
criss-cross red lights, metal implements,
battlefields: birth is always bloody.[2]

I spent a summer working on two poems. I set lines on two facing pages in my notebook, pasting them in: the drafts that would become "Translated Lives" and "Gold Horizon." As I worked my way through the lines, crossing out, adding, fixing a line or image, allowing the breath to flow better, I felt I was inching through a palimpsest of paper, battling with shadow selves, dealing with psychic graffiti—edgy, jagged characters scrawled on a city wall, spawned from lives forced to make up history

On a draft of "Translated Lives" I scribbled a note:

> Rimbaud's Saison en Enfer is much in my mind and also the condition of these immigrant lives we lead and what it means to write (= to translate) across a border—a trip wire. How to summon this up and say, "this is my past, our past: the great challenge as I see it."

I initialed and dated the note, wanting to fix it in the unstable realm of poetic composition: *MA July 15, 1996.*

But what does it mean to stumble on a trip wire, a migratory border? My mind moves to the metamorphosis European sailors feared so much. Traveling east on the waters of the Atlantic some dreamed of an invisible line not far from the Cape of Good Hope. On the other side their bodies would grow dark, sprout horns, oddments of hair, a rare bestiality reserved for those who cross borders.

Spatial transgressions work differently for us now, migrants westwards. The poems we compose, spin themselves out in a cocoon of cold air, inventions born of unvoiced need, and our layerings of self make up a dark soil that we can recall best in dreams. It is a kind of imaginative difficulty for which ordinarily we have few words, a condition of spiritual poverty, lives lived in a world without a readily available history. So fragmenting the self into two, three, we invent what we need: a raw theater of sense. We carry the fear of those sailors within us: but changed beyond recognition. What we are in our bodies becomes fierce, raw, fragmented. Our skin becomes a shield. We tremble to touch.

When Rimbaud mused "Je est un autre" or scribbled thoughts on the "dérèglement" of the senses, little did he know the power his lines would exert on us, we who understand however fitfully that desire is always for the Other, the Other who forces us into history. And it is precisely this entry into history that lets us see the condition of our migrancy, our days lived out in the vivid air, cut from the dream of a steadfast home.[3]

In the aftermath of September 11, 2001, I composed a cycle of elegies. In those days I would keep walking down to Lower Manhattan, to the edge of Ground Zero. After the pain and shock we all went through, it was a delight to read Lorca's *Poet in New York* and try to reattach myself to place through some, and I stress *some,* of his words. At times his voice startled me—"If it isn't the birds/ covered with ash . . ." (*Si non los parajos/ cubiertos de ceniza . . .*). I carried his poems with me as I rode on the subway, and as I wandered about Central Park. One afternoon I sat in Sheep's Meadow with a friend who read out the Spanish lines to me. Listening to him, I felt that Lorca was speaking to me. Lorca had come as a visitor to this island and then left. I had come exactly fifty years later and stayed on. Then it happened, I started to hear Lorca's voice as I walked about the city. His voice in my ear. My response became "Color of Home," "Casida of a Flowering Tree," and "Central Park Carousel": they make up the poem cycle "Listening to Lorca."[4]

In my mother's house in India, by a window that looks out onto a sandy courtyard, there's a bookshelf. When the monsoon rain is heavy, the window by the bookshelf has to be latched shut, to keep out the rain. The books on this shelf, all poetry, help me to discover what it means to come home. Some were collected by my sister Anna who is a poet and painter, some I brought back from my travels, some belonged to my grandmother Eli. So many poets I treasure, their books on that white painted shelf— Tagore, Kumaran Asan, Whitman, Wordsworth, Mirabai, Milosz, Octavio Paz, Neruda, Akhmatova, Kamala Das, Jayanta Mahapatra, Dom Moraes, Keki Daruwalla.

I find the tattered copy of Milosz's *Collected Poems (1931–87)* and search out the powerful, exquisite "Bypassing Rue Descartes." My breath stops when I read the lines,

> There is no capital of the world, neither here nor anywhere
>   else,
> And the abolished customs are restored to their small fame
> And now I know that the time of human generations is not
>   like the time of the earth.

How did I come to Milosz? Almost a quarter of a century ago, when I was new in America, I lived briefly in Minnesota and a writer friend introduced me to Milosz's *Native Realm*. Read it, she urged me.

So that is where I began and recognized immediately his eloquence, the voice that touched the timbre and heft of a century where we are forced to shift continents, turn languages on our tongue, till we finally come to recognize the whole earth as our home. There is a native realm, a psychic space that keeps us from harm and he knew that.

Later in a St. Paul bookstore, I found a beat-up paperback, a collection of essays by various hands about the experience of immigration. It included an essay by Milosz. Again and again I read that essay. He seemed to be speaking to me very personally, saying—yes there is a way to come as an immigrant to America, come carrying your life in your hands, live out your life here, be a poet.

In my New York City apartment I keep a copy of his *Collected Poems* twin sister to the book that sits in my mother's house. My eyes fall on the line from the poem sequence "The Separate Notebooks."

I did not choose California. It was given to me.

I think to myself—it is by grace that I am here. I did not choose this place, it was given to me. Milosz's poetry does its slow, enduring work, enters my inner life. I met his poetry only after the prose, but once I came upon the poems, a music started to work inside me: a translated tongue, a restless permanence.

One poem he composed directly in English—"To Raja Rao." In Hyderabad I had met Raja Rao, spent some hours talking to him. We sat one rainy afternoon on a veranda taking tea and talking. I knew and admired his works, particularly the *Serpent and the Rope*. In those days I had never seen America and wondered how he could live in Texas, what I thought to be the Wild West.

In Milosz's poem for Raja Rao there were lines that stuck in me like thorns, a hurt, an irreparable discomfort:

> For years I could not accept
> the place I was in.
> I felt I should be somewhere else.

A city, trees, human voices
lacked the quality of presence.
I would live by the hope of moving on.[5]

What might it mean to move on? One crossing is irreparable, other crossings are smaller deaths. August 14, 1998, was the day my father died. I am melancholic on that day and often feel in touch with presences beyond our own. My father loved the Bible and would read from the Psalms and also from the New Testament, Corinthians for instance. Milosz died on that very day, six years later. I was filled with emotion. I tried to imagine the poet in Kraków. I needed the ties that bind, other poets who had met him, known him.

I wrote to a poet friend who lives in New York: *I have just returned from India and heard of Milosz's death. He was such a great poet . . . Kerala was filled with monsoon rain.*

On the same day he replied, telling me of a poetry seminar he had taken part in, in Kraków, devoted to Milosz's work. Suddenly the city where the great poet had died seemed not so very far away. I imagined Kraków filled with chestnut trees. Why chestnut? Was it something I had read in Milosz? I could not be sure. In the days that followed in New York I wrote the elegy "August 14, 2004." The whole poem took a day and a half to write. I cut and pasted the pages I had written into my black spiral notebook and tucked it into my bag and took it with me to Skopje. I was traveling there for the Struga Poetry Festival.

The first evening in Skopje a group of us went to have a drink in a restaurant not far from the hotel where we were staying. Across from where we sat was a city square. It was made of concrete and seemed utterly bare. Someone spoke about the earthquake that had destroyed the center of the city.

I would like to see Mother Theresa's house, I said to one of the poets from Skopje and he led us there, pointing out the place where the house once stood. The house, like much of the city, had been razed to the ground in the earthquake of 1963. We moved closer and saw the dark metal inserts in concrete that measured out the span of the tiny dwelling where Mother Theresa was born. It was dark and I stepped forward, carefully.

In the center of the space lay a mass of skin and bones, a child, her pale hair picked out in the streetlights.

A child unhoused, come to where a shelter once stood. She lay there, asleep in the cold air, her thin clothing flapping in the wind. In the days that followed, as we traveled to Ohrid for our poetry readings, I thought of that girl lying exposed in the night air. I returned to the elegy I had composed. I wanted to give it to someone who knew Milosz, someone in his city. Through the Macedonian PEN Association I got the poet Adam Zagajewski's email address. At Chateau de Lavigny, in Switzerland, we had met briefly and I felt he was the right person to send the poem to. Zagajewski was very kind and wrote back: "Now you have to come to Krakow and see the place!"

I thought of how composing the elegy had returned me to the Bible, in particular the first Epistle of Paul to the Corinthians. I had a vivid image of someone with her face covered in silk. And she or was it he was reading out loud: *Though I speak with the tongues of men and of angels, and have not love, I am become as sounding brass or a tinkling cymbal. And though I have the gift of prophecy . . .*

This came to me with such force because as my grandfather lay dying, people took turns to read from the Bible, at his bedside, day and night.

NOTES

1. This poem was published in *Stone Roots* (New Delhi: Arnold-Heinemann, 1980).

2. The poem was published in *River and Bridge* (New Delhi: Rupa, 1995; Toronto: South Asian Review Press, 1996).

3. Under the title "Psychic Graffiti" this third section was published in *Performing Hybridities,* ed. May Joseph and Jennifer Fink (Minneapolis: University of Minnesota Press, 1999). The poems "Translated Life" and "Gold Horizon" were published in *Illiterate Heart* (Evanston, IL: TriQuarterly Books, Northwestern University Press, 2002).

4. Under the title "Listening to Lorca" this fourth section was published in the Festival Catalogue, Poetry International 2002, Royal Festival Hall, London, June 2002. The poem cycle was published in *Raw Silk* (Evanston, IL: TriQuarterly Books, Northwestern University Press, 2004).

5. The quotations from Milosz's poetry are taken from Czeslaw Milosz, *Collected Poems (1931–87)* (New York: Ecco Press, 1990), 383, 349, 226.

Muse

For those who write poetry there is nothing like the particular species of energy the activity brings, a very special pleasure—a whole world of thought and feeling that could not otherwise exist. Poetry is knowledge, a first knowledge that allows us to crystallize the chaotic press of experience, illuminate, if only for a moment, the dark horizon of our lives.

The shape of the world keeps shifting and it is into and out of the world that the poem works its sense. Time becomes us and the poems that we compose are part of the fragile compact we make with history, part of the precarious balance of our interior lives. To compose a poem in this manner of reckoning makes the act an intrinsic portion of a phenomenology of the real.

I wrote a poem "Muse" as part of a cycle called "Notebook," poetic reflections on the act of composition which I published in *Illiterate Heart*. In a note I wrote—"In this cycle of poems I have tried to catch something of the internal architecture of sense, the objects of our metamorphic life—a trajectory from the pitch of memory to the possibility of a shared existence. Yet I am haunted by what my words can barely mark, what for want of a better term I invoke as muse, that invisible space where meaning is made and unmade."

Now it is quite true that I meant what I said, but it is also true that the muse I write of comes to me not as nothingness, but as an Indian schoolgirl, dressed in a dark blue pinafore with shoes and socks. A girl child who must learn. There is something utterly simple about her appearance. She is just there. She has nowhere else to go. She carries her pencil box and book in hand. She learns words that turn for her into a dictionary of desire, single words, *girl, book, tree*. She learns them both in Malayalam and in English.

When I said she has nowhere to go, I meant it, for it is only through being thrown into the world, through being there, that she is able to fulfill her task. I think the lines she whispers in my ear, "Write in the light / Of all the languages / you know the earth contains" came to me by themselves, came first and stayed with me as a haunting melody. And the rest of the poem came and wrapped itself around. Then too the child who speaks these lines to me is also my sole self, cast back in the mirror of time. She comes as a schoolgirl who traveled long and hard, across continents. She has swum through many languages, several of which she could scarcely understand. Yet the light of the sentences she reads marks her for life. Even now, as I write, it is as if I swim in an English into which many other streams pour their waters.

There are two earlier poems I have called "Muse." They appear side by side in the volume of poems *River and Bridge*. In each poem the female figure is unhoused, quite marginal to the world she comes from. In the first poem she is glimpsed as a grown woman, "a form of fire." She kneels by a river and on a bald stone, cuts glyphs. In the second poem the muse is furious. She has nowhere to be. Her sari spills off her flesh. Her flesh is burned with words. Her language is in ruins.

Somehow I had to wait many years to make another poem called "Muse," to make reparation. Another poem, a third poem if you will, that allows the traumatized figure of the woman to metamorphose into a child, a child who shines in an interior space where meaning is made. The words the child gives me are first words, the beginning of things, not their ending.

Muse

I was young when you came to me.
Each thing rings its turn,
you sang in my ear, a slip of a thing
dressed like a convent girl—
white socks, shoes,
dark blue pinafore, white blouse.

A pencil box in hand: *girl, book, tree*—
those were the words you gave me.
Girl was *penne*, hair drawn back,

gleaming on the scalp,
the self in a mirror in a rosewood room
the sky at monsoon time, pearl slits,

in cloud cover, a jagged music pours:
gash of sense, raw covenant
clasped still in a gold bound book,
pusthakam pages parted,
ink rubbed with mist,
a bird might have dreamt its shadow there

spreading fire in a tree *maram.*
You murmured the word, sliding it on your tongue,
trying to get how a girl could turn
into a molten thing and not burn.
Centuries later worn out from travel
I rest under a tree.

You come to me
a bird shedding gold feathers,
each one a quill scraping my tympanum.
You set a book to my ribs.
Night after night I unclasp it
at the mirror's edge

alphabets flicker and soar.
Write in the light
of all the languages
you know the earth contains,
you murmur in my ear.
This is pure transport.[1]

NOTE

1. From *Illiterate Heart* (Evanston, IL: TriQuarterly Books, North-western University Press, 2002).

Translating "Passion"

Fahmida Riaz and I met on a cold snowy day in February, in Ithaca, New York. We were participating in a symposium at Cornell University called "Cartographies of the Vernacular: Directions in Contemporary South Asian Literature." I knew her as one of the foremost contemporary poets of Pakistan. I was immediately struck by her vivacity, the way in which her words caught fire. After I read my poem "Passion," she told me she would like to render it into Urdu.

Her first email, dated Monday, March 13, 2000, was addressed to me in wonderfully idiosyncratic fashion:

> Dear Meerakashi,
> Reached Karachi, would love to have a copy of your collection of poetry. You promised to send me this poem you read at Cornell. Please send it to me by post as I want to translate into Urdu.

Our email correspondence, for a little over two weeks, was brief, intense, focusing in the main on the translation of this poem.

> Date: Sunday, March 26, 2000
> Subject: Re: book
> Dear Meena,
> I got your book. Thanks and thanks again. I've already translated your poem. the first draft. What a wonderful description of a certain state which seemed indescribable! ok. when you say "No words for her. no bronzes" etc. Here, actually "bronzes" also mean prizes. did you also mean that? will write to you again, but do let me know about this point. I have written uske liye na koi lafz, na kansi ke tamghe, na dawatname.
> Yours,
> Fahmida

Sunday, March 26, 2000
Dear Fahmida, sister poet,
So glad the book [*River and Bridge*] reached you. One never knows with packages somehow. Yes, with "no bronze, no summoning" I meant no plaques of commemoration, no high call, and not even words, for there, that place, un-nameable. Just now I'm trying to write a poem having as its setting (or one bit of the setting) the border between India and Pakistan—a little poem about the pity of war. Shall send it to you when it's done.
Affectionate regards
Meena

In the email that follows, the questions and answers are compacted together, and I have kept that form, needing to give a sense of the flow of our back and forth. My responses, which she has included in her email, are in boldface.

Monday, March 27, 2000
Subject: Re: book
Dear Meena, thanks for your reply.
About "passion," it has a number of meanings. it can't be translated as "ishq" . . . is it best to translate as a kind of forceful feeling.
what word of hindi would you think of?
I have written "bala khez." We write " Ishq-e-balakhez" for passionate love.

The word passion I took really from the passion of christ who hung on the cross and died. so it does have a liturgical sense (of intense suffering) but also for me, the passion—as in sexual passion—plays into it I guess, that place where all the elements meet when we overstep the borders. (also Bergman has that movie I love called "The Passion of Anna")

but here I've only used bala khez.
Also, in the last two lines you have played on the english pronoun "I."
It can not be translated as it is. But I will try to convey the meaning through some other means. So what do you say to that?

**Yes, I do think you have to play around with it, since the
sound is supreme here. Ai—the Malayalam cry of pain,
aaiou
eye—in English
and of course "I" (self) also aye as in yes in English . . .
how we are compacted here . . .**

Please do send me your poem. everything seems so bleak
right now.

**I will send you the border poem when I finish it, working on
a few poems now as I seem to do, these things go in bursts**

Tuesday March 28, 2000
Dear Fahmida
It's a cold, rainy day. tight green buds on the leaves. a little
fog. there is a gathering of south asians to protest police
brutality—an unarmed black man was shot 41 times, as he
stood in his doorway. a dark doorway. I feel my soul is there.
I said I would write a poem for the occasion and read it. So
let the words come, in fire. One must hug the green tree as
the words come, so the body is not burnt. I was very moved
by your poem that you read about the adulterous couple
being stoned and the man bending over the woman
to protect her. will you send it to me?[1]
love
meena

Wednesday April 5, 2000
My dear Fahmida,
I have never done this before, emailed a poem just the
minute it was finished. But this is the poem I mentioned
earlier. You wanted to see it and I feel it the right thing to
send it through this immaterial medium, across the borders.
As poets we write in such loneliness and I wanted to share
this with you. I think it has the sorrow and pity of war in it.
Let me know what you think.
With love
Meena

I was anxious about sending the new poem that way. Naked,
through the Internet. No cover, no crib sheet. I hoped Fahmida
would like it. Her reply came ten days later.

Saturday April 15, 2000
Dear meena,
got your poem. liked it?
I wept when I was reading it.
I'm writing a paper on "shared dreams and metaphors"
that I will be reading in N. Delhi on 27th of April in the
SAARC writer's conference. I hope you don't mind that I'm
beginning the paper with your poem. "Passion" has been
translated into Urdu.
A literary journal "Aaj" is planning to bring out an issue on
women. I want this poem to be published in it.

The very same day, April 27, 2000, at a meeting of Arts Initiative for South Asians, a gathering of young writers and artists at Smith College in Massachusetts, I spoke a little of our lives, lived across borders, and of my email conversations with Fahmida. Then I read out the poem with its long, prefatory title: "For a Friend Whose Father was Killed on the Lahore Border, in the 1965 War Between India and Pakistan."

I think back to the time when I composed the poem "Passion." In writing it, I felt I was evoking a condition where words did not easily attach—a state I had read no poems about. I wrote it in Manhattan, seeing what I could out of my high window.

Yet I was translating into the landscape of the small town in Kerala that I come from, and out again, into the space of the page, using the concrete and palpable present as an invisible frame. And perhaps, in the act of translation, the emotion that underpins the words of the poem on the page structures another consciousness, another language, even as discrete lines slip away. A figure of eight, the strip of silk turned wrong side up, then swirled back again to the smooth gleam: what the composition of poetry takes for granted, translation renders explicit, sense crystallized through the seizures of dislocation.

Even as I work on this essay, I am putting the finishing touches to a poem in my notebook. It is about the death of Amadou Diallo, an innocent young African immigrant, who was brutally shot to death by the police as he was standing in his own doorway.
Making the poem, I had to absorb the young man's traveling—

from Guinea, on the west coast of Africa, to the Far East, where his father was a trader in gemstones and Amadou studied English, all the way to the north, to Manhattan, where the twenty-two-year-old met his death. I try to brood on a world in which a new immigrant must live without a palpable history, where all one is turns into a dark silhouette in a doorway.

I read out a draft of the poem standing on a flatbed truck, on a street in Jackson Heights, Queens, at a meeting organized by a group of young South Asians: Indians, Pakistanis, Bangladeshis, Sri Lankans, Desis for Diallo.

There were police on the sidewalks, a few on the rooftops across the way, and something I had never seen, a police helicopter circling overhead. Twice it looped around, in the blue air, in the cold wind. That gathering, organized by young people who in the main had grown up in America, was an important event for many of us, immigrants in a world where we must invent a history, fabricate a dwelling in shared space.

I began with this correspondence between Fahmida and myself because it reveals how one can touch others, move across borders, indeed even fraught national borders, and across linguistic boundaries—in this case, using as a raft the material corpus of a poem, a poem that is being translated from English into Urdu. And this brief correspondence between two women poets, more than a half-century after the Partition of India, is made possible by a cyber-geography, the seemingly instantaneous back and forth of words, zipping through ether.

There is a curious fit here, for me, with what it means to translate. An art of negativity, translation seems to me analogous to the labor of poetic composition in precisely this: the reaching beneath the hold of a given syntax, beneath the rocks and stones and trees of discernable place, in order to make sense.

NOTE

1. Published in *Connect: Art, Politics, Theory, Practice* 1, no. 1 (Fall 2000), special issue on translation. The poem for Amadou Diallo that I refer to was published under the title "The Color of Home" in *Paterson Literary Review* 30 (2001).

Why Venice?

In *Quickly Changing River,* I have a cycle of poems set in Venice. Somehow that ancient city charged with water has become very important to me and I keep traveling there so I can sit at the water's edge in silence. Then, if the spirit moves, I pick up my pen and write. In Venice, I always have my notebook with me. In New York, as I travel the subways and buses, I am less organized, often turning to tiny scraps of paper I place in my purse so that I can jot down things that strike me. I stick the scraps, if they seem important enough, into a notebook, and then take it from there.

In March 2005 the Mondadori bookstore had organized an Indian festival and I was invited to read. I ended up reading a few of the Venice poems I had written. I read the poem "Dog Days of Summer" that had just been published by the *Harvard Review.* After the reading, the very first question asked by the organizer of the event, threw me. It was straightforward enough, but I was at a loss of words to respond.

Why come to Venice?

That was the question I was asked.

All sorts of thoughts fluttered through my head. I no longer recall precisely what I said at that time, but when I came back to my high room by San Marco, I sat up late into the night, writing in my notebook. And this what I wrote, though in truth I no longer recall the emotions passing through my mind as I wrote.

Why Venice?
Because I think of Venice as a third place, as the mouth of the east and the lips of the west.
Because the Nile is cleft from me and the Ganga flows through golden mustard flowers I can never reach.

Because centuries before I was born Marco Polo came to the Malabar coast.

Because as a child I drank water from canals and traveled in black canoes.

Because sitting on the stone steps the other day, I saw my ancestors and they had all turned into pigeons fluttering down into San Marco.

Bit by bit, the slow waters rose.

The lagoon waters rose to make a fountain filled with waves.

Those waves were filled with voices.

And under this, the next day, sitting at a computer at the University of Venice Ca' Foscori, looking out onto the brilliant Zattere, I added three more lines.

I think of myself as a woman who has no place to call her own and the bird I heard in the mango tree in grandfather's garden sounds again, warbling through water.

What might it mean to belong, anyway, when the streets are filled with water?

Venice makes me ask this question.

NOTE

Written in my notebook Venice, March 13, 2005.

The poem "Dog Days of Summer" was published in my book *Quickly Changing River* (Evanston, IL: TriQuarterly Books, Northwestern University Press, 2008).

Gandhi Fields

From the end of October 2000 through January 2001 the eminent Malayalam language writer Paul Zachariah and I wrote back and forth to each other in cyberspace. We had met at an event at the Kerala Center in New York where Paul, Shashi Tharoor, and I read together. During the writing of these emails Paul was traveling through Africa, and though he was hoping to, he never reached Sudan, where I had lived as a child. I was on the island of Manhattan. What follows is a portion of our jottings in cyberspace. I have given each of us the first initial of the last name. I am A, he is Z.

October 31, 2000
Dear Z
Somehow your writing speaks very directly to me. I wonder where you are now. I have in front of me a Chinese book "The Travels of Minglaotse" with these lines: *I have seen the sea three times changed into a mulberry field and back again.* Perhaps some day we will meet again.
Yours
A

November 1, 2000
Dear A
Thank you for listening to my stories. The new poem you autographed for me floats lightly like a bird and the images shimmer. I am only getting into the book. I wonder if you know how wary I am of poetry. I approach it like a cunning wolf. I go to Durban on Friday and wander the Gandhi fields from there.

November 9, 2000
Dear Z
I am thinking of writing a poem on cosmopolitanism. If I
offer it to you perhaps you will sniff at it. If you tear at it with
your teeth it will turn to mist and air in your hands. I feel I
need to go on a pilgrimage, enter another life. Perhaps I am
already at the portals. Please do write and tell me about your
travels. I think of you, as I read Gandhi these days. Without
his travels in South Africa he would never have come to an
understanding of the horror of Untouchability. Then that
incident on Tolstoy farm where he cuts off the hair of the girls
and says something like "the hand that is writing about this
incident cut off their hair." Why did he need to punish the
girls? I wonder how it sounds in Gujarati. I want to write a
poem about this, but I have never seen Tolstoy farm. Did you
go there? If you describe the grass and the trees and earth and
the buildings if any, perhaps I can write the poem. Or tell me
the color of the sky. Yes?
A

November 12, 2000
Dear A
I could not go to Tolstoy farm because of poor planning and I
am in Gaborone, Botswana now. But I have half-a-mind to go
back. Let me see. I went to Pietermaritzburg railway station
where he was thrown out of the train, the wharf in Durban
from where he was led along the street by a mob of white
men, beating and kicking him, Phoenix where he started a
printing press and a small enclave. The sky all over South
Africa is unbelievably vast, a gigantic cupola where Salvador
Dali seems to have painted in clouds. It gives the sensation
that you can just reach and touch it. The velds roll on into
infinity along rolling hills and the sky connects with it all
around in the circular horizon. It is almost always blue and
full of the most extraordinary luminosity. At any given time
there, at least a dozen different countenances to it in terms of
color, cloud-shapes, rain-clouds, thunder clouds, etc. It gets lit
up simultaneously in all kinds of colors. The wind plays a part

in making it a kaleidoscope. It is almost never a brooding sky but full of crazy clouds. The earth in Phoenix Farm was very sluggish, tired and indifferent. Someone had burned down the farm and it has been rebuilt. There were a lot of charred things lying around. All around is a huge squatter's colony of poor blacks from whom it has been now protected by barbed wire. Trees were not lively, even though the mango trees were full of fruit, but they looked uninspired, as if they didn't care. The rebuilt buildings including Gandhi's little house have that newly painted look which makes it all very unreal. Get well and stop thinking dark thoughts. think electronic thoughts!

November 13, 2000
Dear Z
I was so glad to hear from you. And thank you for describing Gandhi country to me. I love the way the real world gets stuck into what you write, whereas with me, I sometimes feel, it's all smoke on water. But why should the lyric voice vaporize the world? I feel I need a new way of making poems. Tomorrow morning I will walk by the river and start a new poem. It will be my journey on this island, while you are traveling a whole continent. I want to make a journey deep into memory, with the rocks and stones and trees showing me the way. This is such a turbulent period in my life. I have a great longing to go home, and somehow hearing you speak Malayalam meant so much to me. It is the language of my dreams you know, in so far as dreams have words and not just brilliant colors, dark doorways, burnt crevices. That poem, I attached to the end of the last email I sent you, "Searching for Porta Santa," my kitchen table poem, did you find it? If not I can send it again.

There's quite a tamasha here, with the votes for president. They're counting the votes all by hand, in Florida. Some of the ballot boxes may be bobbing up and down in the sea. Are you inland now? Or by the water? In Khartoum I was so near the Nile, it's a great river which you will come upon before too long. I hope you have good shoes, and shelter and warmth.
[Text of "Porta Santa"]
Yours A

Porta Santa

You bought rolls of bread so hot
they might have been stones from my childhood.

I followed you, twisted my ankle
fainted an instant, losing body.

Then someone whose hair glows in the dark
led me to a grove of olive trees.

I turned back to the Arno
I saw the blue Giotto saw

I wept at stones
that stored so much light.
*
So where are you now?
In the transparent phone booth in Fumicino airport.

In the crush of those forced to draw metal carts
piled with folded paper, precious scraps of clothing.

Outside on the runway beyond our darkened palms
jets hover, wings filled with sparks.
*
And the door you led me through?
Porta Santa

beside the room where I could not sleep
beside the street named for the serpents

beside the blind beggar covered in sackcloth
—Vieni, vieni, qui—

terrible guide
what would Dante have made of you?

Door of water, door of earth
mirror of gold

I stepped through
hearing the voices of pilgrims cry

Who will melt swords down,
fill courtyards with grain?
*
My soul naked, unashamed
watching from a distance

the body, old sari
washed with blue soap

folded with care, set on a stone
Giotto painted beside a laughing shepherd boy.
—(Poem published in *Raw Silk,* 2004)

November 20, 2000
Dear A
Nice to hear from you. The poem has a shining and trembling
quality about it, as if it's going to spill over like a cascade. But
it doesn't and creates a lovely defense. Thanks for letting me
read it. . . . I am stuck in Harare for no reason. I hope to get
out of here for Mozambique on Thursday. The difficult part
of the journey is slowly approaching I can see.

November 28, 2000
Dear Z
Thank you for reading the poem and for speaking to me
about your own life. It's a hard business but one must dance
over the faults in the earth. Art allows that. A wild and crazy
dance sometimes. Take care of yourself on this great journey.
   I am making quite a few poems but feel quite useless with
prose. What is the weather like there? And what do you eat?
And drink? I sound so naive, even to myself, as if I have never
been near Africa though I spent so much of my childhood
moving between Khartoum and Kerala, each year. It was so
misty last night I could hardly seen three feet ahead, and the
trees at the side of the street looked like houses with cavernous
doors.
A

November 30, 2000
Dear Z
Tomorrow I shall take a walk in the Lower East Side, at the
edge of this island in search of a doorway. I want to write a
poem called "Porta Oscura" about a dark door. To put by the
side of the "Porta Santa." When it is finished, who knows it
may take a month or two, I shall send it to you. Perhaps by
that time you may be near the Sudan. (You must see the

ancient Christian churches of Ethiopia and Eritrea.) Take
care, you are in my thoughts, Yours
A

December 2, 2000
Dear A
Did you go to the end of the island looking for the door that
you want to find? I should love to read porta oscura. Do not
get put off by prose, it gives one a lot of inner form. My date
of birth is June 5 which makes me an unstable Gemini and a
child of sorrow. but I really am not sorrowful. I am trying to
go to Nairobi on Tuesday, till then taking it easy in Harare.
Take care. Do you pray?
Z.

December 3, 2000
Dear Z
You ask if I pray. I think I need deeply to pray. I am in search
of a place that will hold me.

I have found the porta oscura, it is at the entrance to a
desolation, what was a garden torn down in the haste of the
city to gentrify, money rushing in, tearing down green. Its on
the Lower East Side of Manhattan, not far from the East River.
It is there under the teeth of the machines that turn over
earth. And on a brick wall to the left, a painting in green of a
mother and a dark child, entering America. Behind them the
image of a green card, passport to this world. Beneath them
words in Spanish I must go back and write down. There is
metal all around that place to guard it from squatters.

What does it mean to have residence in this earth, our
earth? This is the question that haunts me. To live somewhere,
anywhere. And perhaps the poems are prayers, wings folded.

There is also a little church nearby I must go and try to
enter, black pointed roof, steps. On the outside it says
"Orthodox Catholic of the Hispanic Rites" and I wonder what
that means.

I was born on 17 February in Allahabad, but my mother returned to her home in Tiruvella very soon after my birth. and
she is still there, in that house. and me, I am an Aquarius,

moving and torn and lit. I am so glad that you are traveling. there is nothing quite like that. In my way I am too. yours
A

December 9, 2000
Dear A
I have been recuperating in Nairobi from the Mozambique trip and trying to catch up with my reports. How have you been? It must be terribly cold in New York. Has the river frozen over?

December 11, 2000
Dear Z
How lovely to hear from you. It's a misty day and feels as if the trees and the stones are all swimming in another element. Thank you for your letter. Sometimes I think I write because I don't know how to live, but there you are living and traveling and that gives me courage.

I feel I want to make a geography, a resolute thing of shining images. You ask about the river. No the river is not frozen. It is such a mighty river that the warm water flows under and at most there are packets of floating ice. Perhaps our lives are like that.

I had the most amazing conversation a few days ago with a friend from the Sudan, who I had not seen for 31 years. Her husband is tucked away in Eritrea with the liberation forces of the National Democratic Alliance. She sees him only intermittently. She believes in his work. She and I grew up as children in Khartoum. As she said to me: "Meena, our whole generation is dispersed." So you see my dear how the soil of Kerala within me, stands out like a spit in the sea, and all the bits of land, compacted in the dark waters. My thoughts are with you, yours
A

December 13, 2000
Dear A
Somehow I imagined that the river would be like a white field in winter and people could walk across. There is a great movie

by Kiezlovsky (spelling?) [Kieslowski] where a family is struck by tragedy when their children go skiing on the frozen river and are drowned. I think it is part of his Decalogue.

Someone has offered me a ride into Southern Sudan which is under rebel control. I hope it materializes. but that automatically bars me going to Khartoum/North Sudan. In any case they take four months to issue a visa! So it looks like I am not going to be able to tell you about Khartoum. Let's see.

The Kerala you keep within you is an imaginary homeland. But I always think that imaginary homelands are more creative than the real ones. All writing is finally a game of memory.
Z

December 19, 2000
Dear Z
Its cold here and will probably snow today. I just wanted to wish you a wonderful Christmas and New Year. I do not know where you are but hope and pray that you are safe crossing all those borders.

So it is that we wander into our own lives. I think I am starting a prose book and that is probably quite foolish of me. But there it is. I think there is something quite cussed and obstinate about me, like a child hitting her fist against a stone to prove that she is real, or even swallowing that stone. Affectionate regards, yours ever
A

December 24, 2000
Dear Z
I do not know where you are or even if this email will ever reach you, so in that way you are like the angel I dreamt of as a child, when I was five, on board a white steamer crossing the Arabian sea for the first time. I had left India and I was going to Africa. A form of fire, insubstantial. But of course my friend you are a very real person, even as I am and you are exploring worlds entire, on foot, by road, plunged into another reality. It is very cold here, and I am going away for a few days, taking with me the first notes for a book that begins: "When I was a child I saw the sea burn." It is about that child

158

going to Africa and I wanted to share it with you, that first line which is all I really have. Happy Christmas and have a wonderful new year.
Yours in these electronic flashes,
M

December 26, 2000
Dear A
I am sorry I have been out of touch for so long, but I was traveling somewhat feverishly. I liked the opening sentence of your prose work. I wish you lots and lots of startling and translucent words; also stark words and tender words. Also the special ability prose bestows on you to become cold and analytical while burning from inside. Prose is a great engine you can travel at lightning speeds with and also keep idling as the mind takes off. I am a fool to tell you all this when you know so, so much more. but I am unashamed because it is between two writers. You know what to throw away. . . . What is this place you have found to hide and write? Uganda is an easy place to communicate. Please send me a line when you return.
Z

December 30, 2000
Dear Z
I am writing these words to you from the land of the blizzard of 2000. Everything is snow covered, snow licked, draped and tucked in reams of white. Even the river which one can barely see with the snow flowing down from the sky. Yesterday the river had floes of ice on it, driven from the north and the trees on either side were stark, black with their arms put out. A child might have leapt lightly on all that crushed ice, across to the other side.
It means a lot to me, your words about prose. It helps since I always have the desire to stop, in the way that one does with an image in a poem, rest there, allow the burning to happen. But with prose one has to draw lines forward in a way that I am just learning. So I am still on that ship with the child and the sea water that burns, on the Arabian Ocean, on the way to

the Red Sea and Port Sudan. You see my friend I am making
all these journeys in my head and heart and soon, if all goes
well you will be in Southern Sudan, a place I have never seen.
yours meena
ps when I came in today I even had snow on my eyelashes. I
feel like a snow child.

January 8, 2001
Dear A
Thanks, I am still in Nairobi. The Norwegian group who
promised me a lift into Southern Sudan had problems in the
last minute. The next offer is for February first week, so right
now I am sitting tight in Nairobi and writing out four more
instalments of my stuff for *Mathrubhumi.* They have already
started publishing the material. Later when I get back I will do
a full-fledged one for the weekly. Well, it keeps me busy! I am
leaving for Cairo on the 15th and shall return on the 31st or
so. I remember Cavafy in Alexandria. How have you been? I
have not replied to your last message. . . . I shall soon get back
to you. in the meanwhile take care, write a lot.
Z.

January 16, 2001
Dear A
Where are you and what are you thinking? Many pennies for
your thoughts! Hope this finds you in good cheer. I am in
Cairo and enjoying and respecting this great, beautiful and
intensely human city. And loving it. Your Alexandria is only
three hours away and I shall soon take myself there. There is a
whiff of a chance that I might able to get to Khartoum from
here, but let me not be premature and lose my luck.
    Silence is not good for writers. Do write.
Z.

January 18, 2001
Dear Z
How nice to be talking again, it seems so long somehow. I
found a quote for you. I copied it down from a banner in
the House of Literature in Rome, it's in French by the poet

160

Gérard de Nerval who had the singular distinction of impaling himself on a metal fence—through the throat. He wrote some extraordinary poems. Listen to this, I'll translate it for you: *In time the passion for great travels dies down, that is if you have traveled enough to become a stranger in your homeland.* Its quite a set of lines, no? But Nerval aside I wish I could transport myself like these flickering letters and enter Cairo. It is so very many years since I have been there and I am so happy you are there.

I have a vivid memory from childhood of a street, very narrow, a high wide terrace with white sunlight, and rooms, opening into half darkness. In one room a very fat woman in a colored dress, beckoning someone. She had a waterpot on her hips. There were rugs in the room behind her, the scent of darkness.

Yours

A

Fragile Places

1.

What does it mean to belong in a violent world? It's a question that keeps coming back to me.

The poems in *Raw Silk* were composed in the aftermath of two Septembers—time torqued into a loop, space severs—September 11, 2001, in New York City and September 11, 2002, when I was in Ahmedabad, visiting relief camps for the survivors of ethnic violence.

In arranging the manuscript, I was troubled by what it might mean for a book of poems to draw so deeply on narratives of violence, yet there was no way out if I was going to be true to myself, by which I mean true to that inchoate, utterly voiceless subjectivity that lies buried within, too deep for tears. It is with this part of ourselves that we reach out to others, and in this bodily reaching, lit by the power of the senses, we are allowed to remember. So it is that memory, etched into the visible through beauty, allows us to be reconciled to our wounded, perishing earth.

What follows is drawn in part from the notebook I keep to jot down what comes to me as I write, aspects of the everyday, intrinsic portion of the haunting we call history.

A poem plays in my head, as much for its musicality as anything. Yet its matter is close. My mind moves to another country, to which we are bound in the terrible intimacy of war. But it is not of war, nor of streets filled with the despair that comes in the aftermath of the burning of children instead of paper, of which I wish to think—rather the task of poetry, and what place the poem might have in the wreckage we humans can make of our shared world.

A poem called "Mozart 1935." In it Wallace Stevens addresses the poet: "be seated at the piano." Even if stones are thrown in the streets, even if there is a body in rags being carried out, the poet must sit at his piano. And the lines rise to a magnificence Stevens could muster at need:

> Be thou the voice,
> Not you. Be thou, be thou
> The voice of angry fear,
> The voice of this besieging pain.

I think this poem has been in my head in a hidden buried way all these days. I read it in Khartoum where I first read so many poems that are still important to me. I was in the library by the Nile. There was gunfire in the streets, civil unrest. I was a teenager then and anxious to make sense of the world and only the near mystical twists and turns of the poem could afford me that "starry placating" Stevens evokes.

A month ago, March 2003, I bought two black notebooks. In one I pasted out the pages I was printing of the cycle of Gujarat poems written after a visit to the relief camps there, camps that housed the survivors of ethnic carnage. All the poems including "Letters to Gandhi" had come in an overflow of emotion that kept me from sleep. I needed the security of a boundary, covers within which I could turn pages and take flight from poem to poem.

I had to move back and forth between the poems to make a deeply personal sense out of that chaos. A week or two later I started another notebook which I labeled "Raw Silk" and in that book I set drafts of three poems which also came to me at great speed, a wind-smashed bouquet, pain and grief at the destruction of war, joy in the face of beauty that can sustain us. Some of the images that came to me echoed those that had blossomed in my head in the days and nights of a Delhi winter when I sat in quiet in a patch of sunlight brooding on what I had seen and heard. So into my second notebook I pressed the images that came to me, through layer after layer of sense.

Running my fingers through this notebook I see lines I have written in my squiggly hand. They are lines that tell of how I had tried to make a pure lyric out of the title poem of my new book *Raw Silk* but without my knowing it, a border was crossed.

March 20, 2003
What happens in my poetic production is that almost without knowing it, the violence of history enters in. Creeps in through the back door as it were, enters my consciousness, so that in the poem "Raw Silk" which will be the title poem of the new book I started off by wanting to write a simple poem about a scrap of raw silk that my mother gave me from her mother's sari (and about the mulberry patch my grandmother planted after her return from China) and instead, into that entered the soldiers, the tear gas, the grenades of a childhood in Sudan, just as no doubt in my daughter's consciousness the war (now), the bomb drills in school, all enter in.

Writing the poem I used lines that I emailed back to myself from my office at the Graduate Center. I could then retrieve them at home and work with them. The department printer was not working and I needed typed hard copy, not the edgy scrawl that passes for my handwriting. At home, opening the email with the half-finished lines I sensed that I was in search of an answer to the oldest of questions—Who are you? The lyric is a response.

I searched on the Internet for lines by Enheduanna, the great poet of Mesopotamia, the first poet in recorded history. Afterwards, I could not bear the windowless office I had been given and so I walked up to the eighth floor atrium and opened my eyes and on a high wall saw the Dove of Tanna, Frank Stella's piece filled with light. I had first seen the image, in that way, at that angle, lit by the sun, a week or so earlier when David Harvey had addressed a few of us and listening to his words I turned my eyes to the bright talisman of peace on the wall.

Back in my office I wrote lines in which I felt the beginnings of a poem. Later as I sat and wrote, musing on bombs that burst roofs and walls, a woman poet who did not have the luxury of sitting at her desk and writing, a poet flung out of her home, forced to cross the shattered street. This is some part of the email I sent myself. There is in it some impatience with myself and also some real awareness of the limits of the poem.

> Friday March 07, 2003
> Dear Meena
> you are not so far today. why must you email these messages,
> as if pen and paper were hard to find, or a printer. On the
> Dove of Tanna the artist cut up bits of aluminum and
> painted them over into the dove's tail, the arrow's flight, the
> green bough that signifies the lifting of the waters . . . While
> you're at it why not think of the door you have opened,
> perhaps portal would be a better word, onto the layering of
> fragile places whose petals spurt scents from Paris and
> Istanbul and Rome. Or blood spurting from the cut aorta.
> Wrapping it in raw silk will do no good . . .

The rest of the email contains lines that incorporate what was to come, lines I had to sculpt into shape to make the bare bones of the poem I began in the building where the Graduate Center is housed, 365 Fifth Avenue.

May 18, 2003. I went to the Met to see the First Cities exhibit. The darkness of the silk that draped the walls sent out a pervasive gloom, but the ancient artifacts, bird and spouted vessel and golden ram prancing in a flowering thicket snared the heart.

I found myself in a corner of an inner room and there in front of me was an alabaster disc. Its thickness amazed me, at least six inches in depth, that creamy stone onto which was cut the figure and face of Enheduanna, leading the array of priests, an image I had only seen on the Internet. Without knowing what I was doing I made the sign of the cross, an almost instinctive act I have carried with me from early childhood, a sign I make in the presence of something sacred. As if in a dream I gazed at her face, the cheekbones scooped away, damage hurting her throat but the profile incised there, the hands held out, the precious poem.

I took my dear friend Gauri to face the alabaster disc and I said to her, I will stand here to take darshan. And I stood there for a long time, facing an image of the very first poet in recorded human history. Later I read the poem "Triptych in a Time of War" at an event the students had organized in April at the Graduate Center. As I recall it was the day after the American troops entered Baghdad.

Walking down to Ground Zero on the anniversary of 9/11 we saw twin beams of light shining up into the dark sky and in the beams thousands and thousands of fluttering motes.

Bits of paper? Darting souls?

On 9/11 the air had been filled with tiny bits of paper and ash, all falling, falling. So what was this? These tiny particles were rising, not falling. I asked one of the men who was taking care of the light installation and he told me that they were moths. So moths drawn out of the darkness were glittering, high as the eye could see in twin beams and their delicate wings played in the plate glass of the buildings across the way. The tiny luminous moths made an afterimage that stayed and stayed even after I shut my eyes. The next day, September 12, when a group of us read at Cornelia Street Café, I thought of the souls of the dead, rising in the twin beams of light.

2.

It's a bright spring day, New York City, sunlight in all the places that winter darkness had made us forget, the crook of a wall, the cranny of a tree, tiny rip in an asphalt road and everywhere the sight and scent of spring bursting forth, petals, stamens singing, the joints of leaf and branch rippling with sap and birdsong from behind clouds.

I saw those boughs, that sunlight coming up out of the darkness of the subway, after a meeting in one of the most crowded parts of the city. In a high room a few poets had gathered to talk about Intimacy and Geography. It was a phrase that was meant to encapsulate the theme of an Asian American poetry festival planned for the fall, a phrase that we tossed back and forth, a live ball out of which spilled thoughts of what it might mean to make a home in language, in multiple languages, through exile and uprooting, through migrant memories, fragile places.

Arjun Appadurai has reflected on locality as a structure of feeling. He writes of how the production of locality is "a fragile and difficult achievement . . . shot through with contradictions, destabilized by human motion."[1] Living in place and the crossing of borders are both part of our lives in this century, habitation incomprehensible without the mobility that some choose, and others are condemned to.

More and more our poems are palimpsests of place, memory and desire written through them, the slow darkness of human suffering underpinning their minute and sometimes joyous illuminations.

Theodor Adorno has suggested that the lyric is a form which in its very intimacy, its solitude, is underpinned by the longing of society, for a crystallized structure, a form of feeling that must necessarily refuse that which society stands for, the hard, crowded, oppressive, regulated world—the realms of dos and don'ts. Adorno writes: "This demand however, the demand that the lyric word be virginal is itself social in nature."[2]

Virginal I don't quite understand. But I do understand an intensity that scrubs out the awful constraints in which all that is pure can be trammeled, all that the body can sometimes bind us to, being the creature of place that it is.

I wrote the poem "Passion" evoking the human realms of do and don't—and it was a woman's voice I was thinking of, rising above these, a full soaring note higher, a cry for the place, the paradise only the poem might render possible.[3] So to take that voice, that longing one might move on and think of the poet as one who dwells in fragile places—zones that can be shattered by the raise of a hand, the quiver of an eyebrow, that can be fused together with the fiery power of dream.

I was in India, living in Kerala and teaching as a Fulbright visiting professor at Mahatma Gandhi University, twelve miles from my mother's house. In December I traveled to Santiniketan, in West Bengal, to the university established by the poet Rabindranath Tagore. It was the dry season, cool and dry. I wandered through dusty paths and came upon huts made of wood and thatch, sculptures set in groves of trees, and a marble temple where there was no idol or godhead, rather the spirit, the empty spirit in vacant space that Tagore's father, a Brahmasamaji, invoked. Standing there I saw light streaming through brilliant glass panes onto the cool floor. I felt I could live there, in Santiniketan, the Abode of Peace, for a long long time and it was hard for me to leave.

One morning I closed my eyes and when I opened them again I saw a red bird flying over the museum that houses the artifacts Tagore had collected in his lifetime, the silken robes he used in theater productions, the brocade robes gifted from Japan, the paper on which he wrote, the enamel pen, a model of the train in which he took his last ride from Kolkata to Santiniketan. Even in the rundown parts of his university, I am thinking now of the guest house where wild dogs roamed in the dining hall and pigeons clustered on the bathroom sill, there was his spirit, something set apart from, yet powerfully wedded to the earth out of which he drew his songs. Here are lines from his last set of poems, "Shesh Lekha," the so-called deathbed poems. This was written on May 13, 1941, less than three months before his death:

> On the banks of the Rupanarayan
> I woke
> and realized this world
> was no dream.
> With alphabets of blood
> I saw myself defined.
> I recognized myself
> through endless suffering,
> countless wounds.
> Truth is cruel:
> I love its cruelty
> for it never lies.[4]

Perhaps it is the cruelty of truth that awakens us to the nature of place. Fragile places which we inhabit as human beings, places that we make in order to be persons, in community, in communion, and how very easily that civil pact can be broken, the key to our coexistence tossed away.

3.

September 11, 2002, I found myself in Ahmedabad in Gujarat. The city of Ahmedabad lies on the banks of the river Sabarmati. It is where Gandhi, the father of Indian independence, the creator of nonviolent action, had chosen to set his ashram. In the clear morning light, in the company of a dear friend, I crossed the river over the main bridge. My friend and I found a decrepit three-wheeler that dropped us off in Shahpur, a poor neighborhood. With the help of a Dalit activist—"Dalit" is a term of resistance used by those who were previously called Untouchable—we made our way to a large relief camp, Quraish Hall, that in better times had been used for weddings.

How had this all come about? A barebones telling. In February 2002 a Muslim mob had allegedly torched a train carrying Hindu activists and fifty-nine people lost their lives. The aftermath of Godhra—a single word suffices to summon up that tragedy—was carefully orchestrated by right-wing Hindu groups. The plundering and burning of Muslim properties, the killing and mutilation of men, and the mass rape of women all showed signs of meticulous planning.

As we sat, two women in our cotton kurtas on the low wooden stools in the courtyard, the people pressed around us. They were the survivors of the killings in Naroda Patiya, a neighborhood of Ahmedabad. Svati explained that she was collecting information for PUDR, the People's Union for Democratic Rights, as part of their project of documenting human rights violations. I don't have anything material to give you, Svati said, but please tell us what happened. People pressed forward. There was a terrible hunger to tell their stories.

Afterwards, I could not sleep, hearing those voices. A thin, elderly woman in an orange sari told us how her daughter-in-law Kausar Banu, nine months pregnant, was set upon by armed Hindu men, her belly ripped open, the unborn child pierced by a sword, thrown into the fire. A small dark man, Bashir Yusuf, had survived by hiding under dead bodies. He showed us the marks on his back from knife blades where the Hindutva men had attacked him. He had to run for his life from the Civil Hospital—you are a Muslim, a doctor said to him, I won't help you live.

169

Then a tiny child, barely two, was raised up in the arms of a thin woman. The child's name was Yunus. He was dressed in a torn green shirt, and the woman who was carrying him and said she was his mother turned him around and lifted his shirt and we saw the burn marks on his bottom, where the skin had scarred, the marks stretching over his tiny back, making it look like a raw fruit, terribly disfigured. He had been thrown into a fire and someone had pulled him out and rescued him. The child had enormous eyes and kept staring at me. Even now, back in this wintry city, I see his eyes staring into mine.

Ahmedabad itself was a city split in two. On one side of the river, a thriving city, cars and money and people eating bhel puri on the streets or flocking to restaurants. On the other side of the river, marks of devastation and victims with no means of livelihood filled with fear of what would happen if they dared to return to their old neighborhoods. One thing I cannot forget—when people desperate for help approached the Sabarmati Ashram, those who were in charge of the ashram closed the doors on them, denied them shelter.

I first entered the ashram in what feels like another life, over two decades ago, in the company of Svati's father, the Gujarati poet Uma Shankar Joshi. He was a follower of Gandhi and knew the compound and the buildings well. I followed him into the cool, low-ceilinged house as he showed me where Gandhi and his wife Kasturba had lived. Now in this season of difficulty I felt the peace inside Gandhi's dwelling. I stopped, touched the walls of the small whitewashed kitchen I have always held in memory. Low shelves, windows, small receptacles for food. There was peace here, but at what cost was it maintained?

At the threshold I shut my eyes. I saw the Mahatma, in his pale loincloth. He tore open the doors of the house, he strode down the path under the neem trees. He cried out in words that were hard to understand. He leapt into the river, a flash of flesh and cloth. In bold, unhurried strokes he swam across the Sabarmati. Then, just as he was, Gandhi walked into the burning city.

That afternoon, as always, there were green parrots. I saw them as I walked down the steps of Gandhi's house. They flitted through the trees, into the holes in the outer wall of the ashram. The walls went down all the way to the river.

On the other side of the river innocent human beings had been killed and raped. I watched the parrots disappear into their hiding holes. Slowly it grew dark, then darker. The river, with the smokestacks on the other side, kept flowing on.

What I had seen and heard in Ahmedabad was too terrible for me to tell my mother who was waiting for me in Kerala, five hundred miles away. When I returned I found her sitting, as was her habit, in a wicker chair, looking at the carp circling the lotus pond. As if sensing my disquiet she did not press me too hard. After all she had newspapers and watched TV. Gujarat seemed far away, another country. I felt I had crossed a border, entering Kerala again. But Gujarat was after all part of India and that other locality and its terrible dismemberment was portion of the news of our world.

Later I traveled to Delhi to give a reading at the Sahitya Akademi, the National Academy of Letters. On my first day in the city I went to Bengali Market to buy fruit. I had a great longing to taste pomegranate and this was the right season for them. I felt that before I read my poems I had to eat this fruit with its hard skin, its brilliant red seeds. Though pomegranates are available in many parts of India, somehow I associated them with Delhi, with its red sandstone buildings and brilliant winter skies.

Entering the market I thought I heard the voice I had heard in my head in the days and nights after my return from Gujarat.

It was the voice of the great Russian poet Anna Akhmatova who in her "Instead a Preface" to the poem *Requiem* describes how she stands in a winter street in Leningrad, in a long line of people in front of a prison and a woman recognizes her, a woman with blue lips who comes over to the poet and whimpers, "Can you describe this?" and Akhmatova replies, "I can."

One draws strength from the great ones who have gone before and as I stood in that Delhi street, Gujarat already another place, far away, I heard Akhmatova's words. And I saw in front of me, wrapped up in a khadi shawl and wools, a dearly beloved friend. He was leaning forward in an autorickshaw, a three-wheeler that was about to start. The autorickshaw was parked in front of a tiny storefront clinic, one of many in Delhi that dispense medicines and basic healthcare to urban dwellers. This clinic had a sign in it in big red letters that caught my eye: Dr. Gandhi's Clinic. I went forward and embraced my friend whom I had not seen for many years. I wanted to tell him about my visit to Gujarat but just then there was no time. That had to wait for later. He was Ramu, Gandhiji's grandson. Many months later, back in New York, when I wrote my poems, his voice and figure entered in, restoring time, restoring me to place.

4.

The present is not another country. It is where we live. When I started to write the Gujarat poems, I knew I had to rely on beauty. Otherwise the rawness of what had happened, the bloody bitter mess would be too much to take. The poem can take a tiny jot of the horror but evoke grief, restore tenderness so that we are not thrust back into an abject silence. As if we have heard and seen nothing.

After the poems were completed, I sent them to a friend at the *Times of India* and he in turn sent them onto a friend at the *Hindu* with the thought that they might publish them on the Sunday literary page. So it was that Ranjit Hoskote, poet and editor, wrote back to me. First he spoke of how for many years he had followed my work, then he wrote a few lines about my poems that made me stop in my tracks:

> Dear Meena . . . I . . . am, frankly, amazed by the poems
> provoked by the pogrom and its aftermath in Gujarat, by
> the way they weave terror and disturbance with beauty and
> elegance of form in the way that sometimes makes people
> who are distrustful of the claims of art suspicious of poetry
> and its intentions.

He was a poet himself and I valued his words but what did he mean by the distrust of beauty? He had touched a nerve and I wrote back the same day, March 18, 2003, by email:

> Dear Ranjit, Beauty and terror—we must speak of all that
> sometime. I needed beauty there to work so that the pity of

it would strike the reader. too much horror, raw, the mind
cannot take—and here beauty can work for us, for the
good, so I dare to believe as a poet.

NOTES

Published in *TriQuarterly* 122 (2006). An earlier version of section 3,
under the title "Crossing Sabermati," was published in the *Women's Review of Books,* February 28, 2003.

Portions of this essay were first presented at a talk as part of a series on
the theme of Change, Shippensberg University, April 15, 2003; a version was presented at a panel at Dartmouth College, "Transnational
Ethics and Aesthetics in Asian American Literature," May 1, 2003. The
others on the panel were Maxine Hong Kingston, Garrett Hongo, and
Li-Young Lee. I am grateful to them for the discussion we had.

1. Arjun Appadurai, *Modernity at Large: The Cultural Dimensions of
Globalization* (Minneapolis: University of Minnesota Press, 1996), 198.

2. Theodor Adorno, "On Lyric Poetry and Society," in *Notes to Literature,* ed. Rolf Tiedemann, trans. S. W. Nicholsen, vol. 1 (New York: Columbia University Press, 1991), 39.

3. Meena Alexander, "Passion," in *The Shock of Arrival: Reflections on
Postcolonial Experience* (Boston: South End Press, 1996), 17–20.

4. Rabindranath Tagore, *Shesh Lekha: The Last Poems of Rabindranath
Tagore,* trans. Pritish Nandy (New Delhi: Rupa, 2002), 27.

IV. Poetics of Dislocation

But thought in reality spaces itself out into the world
—Édouard Glissant

Writing Space

A migrant life lived through continents, across waterways and islands creates the space where I write—a space that infolds memory, marking whorl upon whorl of time, mutating palimpsest I have learned to reckon with.

I write in solitude, using the materials of a shared life: pathways of sky and soil and water.

I write on paper pages, or in fitful electronic flashes that appear on a screen, or occasionally with a sharp stick on soil, just as I used to do as a child.

Like many others I cross as best I can ordinary streets filled with the rumor of war, airports decked out with barbed wire, underground places threatened by sudden explosion.

This day-to-day life is scored by the burden of discrepant nationalisms, fevered ethnicities. But it is here and nowhere else that the invisible life goes on, the life of dream and imagination that seeks its sustenance in and through the sensual body.

A woman's body tracked through space, intact and bloodied, drawing out bit by bit in lived time, blossoming words, rare geographies of longing.

Crossing the Indian Ocean

I was with my mother on the S.S. *Jehangir,* crossing the Indian Ocean. Midway on the journey I turned five. Bombay was far behind and Port Sudan still to come. It was my first sea voyage.

Until then I had lived on solid land, on the Indian subcontinent and all my journeys had been by train or car or on small wooden boats on the canals and waterways of the coastal region I come from.

The sea cast me loose.

The sea tore away from me all that I had. In doing so, it gave me an interior life far sooner than I would have had otherwise, but at great cost.

I was forced to enter another life, the life of the imagination.

But it was not as yet the life of language.

I had few words at my disposal, and those I had came from several languages that cohabited within my head. What I felt as a child and held deep within myself quite exceeded the store of words within my reach.

This is something that I feel, even now as an adult. The struggle for words, the struggle to be human, is coexistent for me with the craft of poetry.

On my fifth birthday I was plunged into a world with no before and no after.

A child can fall into the sea, never to reappear.

A mother can appear out of the waves, only to vanish, reappear, and then vanish again.

The sea has no custom, no ceremony. It allows a theater for poetry, for a voice that cries out, that splits into one, two, three or more, chanting the figurations of the soul, marking a migrant memory.

The day I turned five, I stuck my head out through the porthole of our cabin and saw ceaseless water. On and on, until my eyes and neck hurt, I kept watch.

When I pulled my head back in I knew the sea was painted on the inside of my eyelids, would never leave me.

Sometimes the syllables of poetry well up, waves on the surface of the sea, and they burst as flying fish might, struck by light.

Sometimes I feel this is how I began, a wordless poet, a child on the surface of wide water with all that she loved torn from her, cast into ceaseless suspension.

The page on which I write is a live restless thing, soul-sister to the unselving sea.

Threshold City

Time works in us the way water works at the edge of the sea: there are ripples and eddies and the slow sedimentation of earth rounded off by water, sudden slips and plunges where waves crash, and sometimes underwater faults that suck the seawater out and send it soaring into a wall that comes crashing down on small human habitations built by the shore.

Time sucks and blows through us and sends us reeling.

Our bodies become living markers of time. Memory makes us hop and race and dance and flee.

Still, the present is always with us, and our poems transfigure place by marking time.

We write in order to live. We live in order to write.

Poetry marks a threshold, a dream state, by casting time into relief. In this way it spares us and permits our residence on earth.

Ontology can be understood as threshold.

The question of being, of openness to time, is the province of poetry.

Poetry is music that our bodies etch on the provisional solidities housing us, as ground is marked by the shadow of clouds, as unstable ground is constantly etched by water.

The threshold is a city, layer upon layer of brick and stone and painted wood, metal, semiprecious stones, a shield for our impediments, a buckler in the face of death, which is what the city hosts, even as life swarms and spills through it.

Allahabad, Khartoum, Delhi, Hyderabad, New York, cities I have lived in, which set up thresholds constantly overcome, inconstantly wrought as speed manufactures sites for contestation.

The body is a threshold, loved and scarred by other bodies.

We race through cities, past barbed wire, through transit lounges, across borders where memory of the sea dissolves as clouds in a mirror edged with gilt, touched by invisible hands.

Poetry is a threshold inscribing memory.
Memory tunes and untunes us.
It sings the visible and the invisible. The nervous knowledge of the body is raised as sung chords through lungs, throat, vocal chords, palate, tongue, teeth and lips, out into the blue air.

Poetry is a threshold inscribing mortality.
Once completed, the poem is borne to the edges of public space, of history. And there it survives, if it can.
At times the poem is hidden under a pillow, at times trumpeted abroad, at times burned, at times cast into water.

I think of the *Kalachakra Mandala* created by Tibetan monks.[1] Once the painstaking work is completed, the mandala—made of hundreds and thousands of grains of sand—is borne aloft, cast into running water.
When the poem is done, its metrical consonances, its rhythmic images and sharp bounding lines cut loose, leaving us in penury.
We start all over again, searching out the zone where the body's skin and the stones of the city meet, feverish threshold constantly renewed.
Our lines mark out unquiet borders, our words figure a palimpsest of desire, inklings of dark gold in poems of our season.

NOTES

Published in *Contemporary Women's Writing* 1, no. 1 (2007), inaugural issue.

1. The Kalachakra Mandala or Wheel of Time Mandala is a figuration for the blessing of time created by Tibetan Buddhist monks. It is formed by the patient pouring out of many colored sands. Upon its completion the mandala is cast into running water.

In Time

Where does poetry come from? How to answer a question about the provenance of poetry, evoke a most elusive truth?

There are sentences that spell out an answer, lines that I have held onto for their signal power: *I have said that Poetry is the spontaneous overflow of powerful feelings. It takes its origin from emotion recollected in tranquillity: the emotion is contemplated till by a species of reaction the tranquillity disappears, and an emotion, kindred to that which was before the subject of contemplation, is gradually produced, and does itself actually exist in the mind.*[1]

But now I think, what if Wordsworth got it utterly wrong? And what if there were no tranquillity to be had? The poet lays out a picture of a mind in fluent motion, recollection as a boon that permits imaginative contemplation.

But what if instead of an emotion *kindred to that which was before the subject of contemplation* something utterly disparate comes into being, quite apart from what memory grants, and we are faced with two figurations of feeling, one and the other utterly distinct, no dialectic possible and what emerges is the terror of consciousness, fierce sister to the sublime.

This separation of consciousness, a tear or rip in the fabric of time as it is sensed, brings us closer to traumatic knowledge which has no words to fit to its ghostly flesh till the poem flashes, a crystal of words swept high into air, easily shattered.

The poem, as I think of it now, is a fragile crystal of breath; the silence at its core mirroring what was crossed out, mutilated, could never approach the condition of words. A crystal of words luminous in time.

1. William Wordsworth, "Preface to *Lyrical Ballads*" (1802), in *William Wordsworth,* ed. Stephen Gill (New York: Oxford University Press, 1984), 611.

Island City

To build is in itself already to dwell
—Heidegger[1]

I need this city to write in. The thought came to me with the sharpness of a hunger pang, with fierce excitement.

Newly arrived in New York City I was trying to make sense of towers of glass, steel and brick, underground passageways built for speed, overcrowded bridges, bristling sidewalks and all around the island, barely visible, the slow lapping of water from estuary, river, and sea.

I was filled with wonder, how else shall I put it? But this coupled with a sense of shock, a feeling that I had hit ground on the other side of the mirror.

I understood early that to live on this island, I would have to write.

That the writing of poems might permit me to make a shelter for myself. I felt that otherwise, I would have nowhere to be.

It was a familiar feeling for me, a need to make ground, to build a dwelling space with words. The task of making the intricate structure of the poem could allow me space to live.

I found a job in a college that stands above a subway stop, its escalators and elevators packed with immigrant students. I felt I was living at the crossroads of the world.

Sometimes I wandered alone, out into the streets, or sat by myself on a park bench. I saw buildings being torn down, the razing of small community parks, the erection of massive, over-priced condominiums.

I murmured lines I had learned by heart as a child in school in a far country—*la forme d'une ville / Change plus vite, hélas! Que le coeur d'un mortel.*[2]

The electric grid of activity in the city became a scrim for poetry. From time to time elements of my past came to light, but always the here and now of my days and nights in the city made a translucence through which to glimpse the moving figures of the past, those objects and elements of sound and sense that structure the musicality of desire till the poem becomes sonorous space, lightbox of longing, choreography of voice, mortal architecture.

NOTES

1. Martin Heidegger, *Poetry, Language, Thought,* trans. Albert Hofstadter (New York: Harper Colophon, 1971), 146.
2. Charles Baudelaire, "Le Cygne," in *Oeuvres Complètes* (Paris: Editions Robert Laffont, 1980), 63.

V. In Conversation

The Task of Poetry
A Conversation with Ruth Maxey

RM: *What do you see as the task of poetry?*

MA: In a time of violence, the task of poetry is in some way to reconcile us to our world and to allow us a measure of tenderness and grace with which to exist. I believe this very deeply and I see it as an effort to enter into the complications of the moment even if they are violent but through that, in some measure, the task of poetry is to reconcile us to the world—not to accept it at face value or to assent to things that are wrong, but to reconcile one in a larger sense. Camus says in *The Myth of Sisyphus* that there's only one philosophical question: whether to commit suicide. And he says, "the point is to live." He says that we must imagine Sisyphus happy as he pushes the stone up.[1] Seen in that way, the act of writing is intrinsic to the act of living. It's as if Sisyphus has to keep reinventing the wheel: once he goes up, the wheel rolls down and he has to start again. It's a punishment but it's also the way in which he grows in the world.

I would be the happiest being on earth if I could say, "I've written this wonderful book of poems." I wouldn't have to write anymore. I could lie in the sun. Why does one want to blow one's brains out on these bits of paper? It's an enormous psychic effort but there is an amazing clarity that you have for a little while. When you complete a work, you breathe deeply and think, "Oh yes, I've done it!" But then you have to start again.

By finishing one work, one has actually learned something that allows one to go on to make the next. But you don't know that consciously because if you did, it would get in your way, so each time the hope is that you're able to work with the material at hand but perhaps in a slightly different way. But you don't

189

know that up front, that's the discipline you've learned. You have to look away from it. I think the poem is an invention that exists in spite of history. Most of the forces in our ordinary lives as we live them now conspire against the making of a poem. There might be some space for the published poem but not for the creation. No ritualized space that one is given, where one is allowed to sit and brood, although universities give you a modicum of that. Poetry is a forsaken art, not for those who write or practice it, but for many others. Yet there is a kind of redress that poetry offers. I'm using the words of Seamus Heaney, who has a wonderful essay "The Redress of Poetry" in his Oxford lectures, where he talks about poetry as something existing within the gravitational pull of history and yet offering, precisely because of that pull, a redress or a balance.[2] At this moment in my life, this is the very best possible telling or accounting that I have found in all my searching of what it is that poetry does.

RM: *I want to touch on your relationship to Wordsworth. In* Nampally Road, *Mira defends her decision to teach his work in India. I was interested to see that because for other postcolonial writers, the study of Wordsworth in particular is a contested area.*

MA: When I went to the Royal Festival Hall [in London] in 2002 for Poetry International, they asked each poet who our presiding spirit in poetry was, and I chose Wordsworth. And I said, "In picking Wordsworth I have to admit to a pained love that is not easy to speak of, an attachment so deep that I have sometimes felt it would be easier to deny it." And then I asked myself an important question, "Why Wordsworth?" And I answered, "Because his words cut straight to the heart of my childhood—the trauma, the blessing, the interior life the child bears within." And so often that interior life is cut away from the realm of words. Yet I felt that in order to read his work, I had to cross a line of blood. There is, of course, also his notion of the growth of a poet's mind. *The Prelude* was an architecture. He was building this huge unfinished thing when he made *The Prelude*.

So I got this idea that the great poem was a house that was co-extensive with a felt understanding of the self in growth. *The Prelude* was actually critical to this enterprise but then growing to consciousness, I felt that everything Wordsworth stood for was completely inimical to where I'm coming from. In fact, the title poem of *Illiterate Heart* is about meeting these poets—one is an Indian poet, "a mahakavi from the temples of right thought." The other is Wordsworth as I imagine him: "Or one in white flannels / unerringly English, lured from Dove Cottage, / transfixed by carousels of blood, / Dalton's daring, stumbling over stones / never noticing his outstretched / hand passed through me."[3] I wasn't even flesh to that mode of apprehension. In other words, I didn't exist. Yet he was an extraordinary poet.

RM: *You've said that poetry is more crystalline, while fiction and life-writing give you more scope for exploring ideas. How do you see the transition in your work between genres? And does prose allow you to explore more disturbing themes?*

MA: How interesting. It might. On the other hand, the poem "Triptych in a Time of War" [*Raw Silk*] is quite disturbing but it does use longer lines, so it's like a prose poem almost. I think there's a sort of continuum, but what the prose essay or fiction allows me to do is almost like a clearing of the underbrush, going ahead as if you're on uncharted territory, filled with vines, underbrush, wild grass, and rocks, and clearing a space. Then once you've cleared the space, you can do the poem there.

Prose has a different function for me because it's broad, using a different sort of canvas. But once I've done that, there is the poem that I have to make. Then it's also the case that for the book of essays that I'm putting together, I often write a poem and then work from that. In other words, I get to a place in my understanding through the poems, but it's not articulated as such. It's not set out in discursive thought because it's a poem. And then I have to move from that and I can use the prose essay to try and reflect on where this other, new place is. Could I do it without writing prose? Yes, perhaps. I imagine I could. But it's fun to do, it helps me, and also you know in classical Indian writing, there was a tradition of *kavya,* which existed before there was the distinction between prose and poetry. *Kavya* can be a prose poem, highly charged. I think some of the writing in the new edition of *Fault Lines* is like that. These are fluid, unquiet borders for me, because there is traffic both ways.

RM: *That's a helpful way of thinking about it because so much of your work is about migration and geographical borders, cultural borders and thresholds*

MA: I write a certain kind of prose that is, in its texture, closer to the sorts of little knots that an embroiderer uses. The way it works is through an image rather than emplotment.

RM: *Yes, I noticed in* Fault Lines, *for example, that you used very short paragraphs, sometimes only two lines.*

MA: That's something that comes from the poem rather than from a certain kind of prose. I'm not a great plot person. That isn't the way my head works. I work much more with the image in an instant of time and the resonance that it opens up.

RM: *In* Fault Lines, *you speak about "making up memories." To what degree are memories constructed? Is there a deliberately blurred line between fiction and memoir in your work?*

MA: In order to make memoir, you have to make things up as well. Even memories are made up at some level. You remember things but you don't often have the words, so as soon as you start putting the words in place, you're constructing it in the framework of the present. And you have to dramatize certain things and not others. With the memoir it was only when I started writing that I started to remember. It was as if the act of writing allowed a space within which one could remember.

RM: *Can we talk about your relationship with language? I know the idea of heteroglossia is very important in your work: your use of English is informed by Arabic, French, Malayalam, Hindi. How do these other languages form part of your creative process when you're writing in English?*

MA: It probably works at the level of rhythm as much as anything and perhaps also at the level of image because thoughts are given to us at an almost prelinguistic level. They come to you without words; an idea can come to you quite early in life. You pick up certain kinds of possibilities of rhythm from your mother's speech or the kinds of houses in which you grow up, and when the art is accurate it draws on that. Some of my poems have been translated into Malayalam and people have sometimes remarked on how certain kinds of rhythms in a poem are from Malayalam. That may be true, but I can't really read or write Malayalam, though I speak it fluently. My mother tongue exists as orality for me.

So inevitably in the second language that one inhabits—I use that term "inhabits" advisedly—there is a way of making accommodation for what has not yet been thought and I think that sort of accommodation is what a poem allows. I have multiple languages working for me. But I have always grown up in a world where there were things one did not understand, because there were languages that were not completely accessible: you use one language in the marketplace, another in the kitchen, another in the bedroom or the study. And then your friends are those who often speak some of those languages as well and it just gives you a particular sense of being in a world where you can be comfortable even though linguistically the world is not really knowable. I think this is a very good hedge against a certain kind of rational understanding, the presumption of linguistic clarity or transparency, post-Enlightenment, the sense that everything can be known and a light can be shone into all parts of one's thought.

RM: *You have said that "the woman poet who faces the borders her body must cross, racial and sexual borders, is forced to invent a form that springs out without canonical support."[4] What form do you feel you've invented? And what is your position now in relation to the canon?*
MA: It's a very complicated and important question and it's difficult for me to think about. I think the mind is free and one ought to be able to draw upon whatever one needs. Why shouldn't I teach Wordsworth? Why shouldn't I draw on him for what I write? Why should I only draw upon women or women of color? It's ridiculous. There was a time when I read a great deal of poetry by women and it was very important to me to do that. I was fascinated by what it might mean to make poetry as a woman, because there are certain kinds of burdens that form you or that you inherit. They're part of being in a particular body. And not just that, it's also the idea that aspects of what are called or thought of as "canonical literature" are not available to you.

That is a painful knowledge, which is why I wrote my book *Women in Romanticism,* because although there are women poets who are enshrined in the canon in India, or in China or elsewhere, within English poetry of a certain era, certainly, the burden of knowledge has gone the other way. Implicitly the poet was still male. I'm not saying that the development of a woman poet requires that she enter into overt reflections on these issues. But I think it is necessary that she faces them, if only in the solitude of making the work of art. So you cannot evade it even if the artwork in no way overtly relates to it. It is formed within the pressure of a gendered history. There was a time when I had a real quarrel with form in poetry. I'm not there now. I actually value it very deeply. But if you'd asked me ten years ago, I'd have felt that the orality of my experience and particularly an experience which involved a rich, prelinguistic awareness of other languages (and this takes us back to the question of heteroglossia), which is what I wanted to put into my English poems, would have been destroyed had I tried to achieve what we think of as a strict form. So I went for certain kinds of forms which were looser, and coming to America was wonderful for that, because American poetry does have a capaciousness in terms of how form works because vernacular is enshrined in it also.

In that sense, the passage to America has been very important for me as a poet, whereas if I'd gone to England I wouldn't have achieved this. English poetry is much more bound within the canonical tradition, for better and worse. Even as within contemporary American writing there is an idea of a canon, but it's of very recent provenance. If you come from a culture like India or Britain you have an ancient history, whereas America has all the energy and excitement of novelty and the dangers and difficulties of that also. When I came to America, I found the language amazingly liberating. It was very exciting for me to hear American English, not that I can speak it well, but I think in it. It allowed me to make a shift into a different kind of spelling-out of what one might be. That and the idea of being an immigrant. Both of those were very liberating.

RM: *What do you still hope to achieve as a writer?*
MA: I want to write some poems! I keep writing because I'm never really satisfied with anything that I do. It's as if I'm driven from the inside because I don't rest in what I've already written.

I can't. I'm not built that way. And so there is always the next poem. When I was young, I did think a poet should be like Rimbaud. Do one's life's work very young. Now I think of myself as someone who has a whole lot of work ahead of her.

NOTES

This interview took place at the Graduate Center, City University of New York, on February 25 and 28, 2005. Published in *Kenyon Review*, vol. 28, no. 1 (2006).

1. Albert Camus, *Le Mythe de Sisyphe: Essai sur l'Absurde* (Paris: Éditions Gallimard, 1942), 92, 168.
2. Seamus Heaney, *The Redress of Poetry: Oxford Lectures* (London: Faber, 1995), 3–4.
3. *Illiterate Heart* (Evanston, IL: TriQuarterly Books, Northwestern University Press, 2002), 63–64.
4. "Unquiet Borders," in this volume, pp. 80–82.

Bhakti Poetry, Poetry as Transport

A Conversation with Roshni Rustomji

RR: *I think of you as a poet-activist, very aware of the different traditions of Indian literature and especially that of the medieval devotional poets (Kabir comes to mind) who worked to create more just and more balanced societies through their poetry, their songs. And of course Mirabai. It is from this place—the place of bhaktas and bhakti poets—that you begin to think and write.*

MA: You have touched on something critical to my work—that I take root from that wandering, ecstatic woman Mirabai seeking, fleeing, wandering so that she can sing of her love. A love which has no home except for Krishna, her *ishtadevata,* the god one makes through desire. So this longing which burns, burns her out if you wish of the mortal coil, the coil of the domestic, of the ordinary, of the chartered world, allows her at the same time to make her poems, to sing. Of course it renders her unsuited in many ways to what we like to think of as the claims of the world. What she leads us to is poetry as transport.

So there is a simplicity, a grace if you will, in the poetry of both Mirabai and Kabir. A dwelling in the body that does not cut consciousness apart from the desiring, perishing body and sings, sings through sorrow into joy. A precarious joy that remains at the edge of the world. And of course there are the societal implications of this, tossing away the taxonomies of the world, high and low, Brahmin and Sudra, heaven and hell.

Then to return to this question of grace—Kabir as you know enters into "Kabir Sings in a City of Burning Towers," and in the new edition of *Fault Lines,* quite specifically in a chapter called "Lyric in a Time of Violence" I speak of what lay behind the writing of this poem, the aftermath to 9/11, the backlash against brown people, my fear of wearing a sari so that I rolled up my silk in a ball and put it into my book bag and when I unfolded it I thought I saw the eyes of a weaver staring at me and I heard Kabir's voice in my ears.

RR: *There's a question that has haunted poets (and readers) through time and across all the places that form our world. It is a question you echo in a brief sentence in the email you wrote to me: "Of what use is poetry in these times?"*

MA: To be honest, I am gripped at times by despair about the condition of the world. This summer (the summer of 2006) the bombardment of Lebanon and the plight of civilians there was something that haunted me. And what is happening in Darfur is so much in my mind. As you know I spent a good part of my childhood and teenage years in Khartoum and I had friends who came from the Darfur region. Then too, closer at hand with family, with dear ones, the passage of time, the inextricable plotting and cutting up of home and house (I speak of my mother's house and the land around it in Kerala).

Poetry. Why poetry? For me it is profoundest speech. It is a place that human beings go when they cannot do anything else, it is utterance of the dumb, the silenced, the hidden. It is what comes out from both kinds of silence, the transcendent, the visionary which so often finds no habitation in words and that other, that which is crossed out, not permitted to remain, cannot even be retained in memory because it is traumatic, emerging only in flashes of time, breaches of time if you wish.

Yes, poetry is what breaches time, and allows for song. So this is the use of poetry, to reconcile us to the suffering, ecstatic world, not to accept injustice, but to keep our human measure in the face of the inhuman, the degradation, the tearing apart. First and finally—to return to that word bandied about so much, often soiled in our current political discourse—it is our freedom. Poetry is freedom, the freedom of the human soul.

RR: *Why do you write today in the aftermath of the events of 9/11 in New York, a city you know as one of your homes? And I am thinking also about the new, 2003 edition of your memoir* Fault Lines *which you have already spoken of.*

MA: I had never thought of Manhattan as an unsafe place, in spite of what some people think. Its an island city I love, where I have lived and moved and had my being. After 9/11 I wrote three elegies for the dead, making up the cycle "Late There was an Island" and then in the Kabir poem there is pain and anger at the backlash against brown people, and in the Lorca poems which I composed for the Royal Festival Hall in London, the tenderness and passion of a great poet slips into the veins of the one who struggles to write in time present. I wrote the pages I added to the new edition of *Fault Lines* in the aftermath of 9/11 and somehow that attack so close to ground, here where I live, where I gave birth to my children and have raised them, the grief and rage at the waste of it all, came together with the history of my own childhood, something that had come up for me in flashes and threatened to unseat me, and I needed to write of one and of the other and they came together in this space of time.

So that is what poetry does for us, it makes the present come alive, flash up for us, not cut loose from the past but not darkened by it either.

Home, coming home, perhaps this is what poetry does for us, we who are not very easily at home, not even in our own skins.

It etches light on the ground, on the heaving shaking broken ground so we can return home. Where is home? How can I answer that?

It will take me another whole lifetime of writing poems to get there, and even then, of course, it will not be there. And perhaps that is the truth of it, that there is no there, where the question of home is concerned.

Perhaps that's why I love Tiepolo's sketch *The Transport of the Sacred House to Loreto*. It hangs in the Accademia, in Venice. The painting itself was bombed and destroyed in World War II. What we have is the sketch, which itself is such a powerful evocative thing, the house blown in air, through clouds, Mary standing on the tilted roof, her blue cloak opened, the grim old man at the outer edges, holding on for dear life, trying to drag the house down while angels trumpet and blow and raise the house, tiny angels with the faces of impish children, and all the while we know that great crosscurrents of wind are buffeting this frail structure of stone and wood as it rises in the sky, crossing over borders of land and sea, this house of poetry.

NOTE

This conversation was based on several meetings and then continued by telephone and email in October 2006. It is the shorter version of an interview that is published in *Passage to Manhattan: Essays on Meena Alexander,* eds. Lopamudra Basu and Cynthia Leenerts (Newcastle: Cambridge Scholars Publishing, 2009).

Acknowledgments

My special thanks to the John Simon Guggenheim Foundation for a Fellowship in Poetry that freed me to compose my poems and also complete the writing of this book. Thanks to the Camargo Foundation for three wonderful months filled with work at the edge of the Mediterranean Sea.

Grateful acknowledgment is made to the editors of the publications in which these pieces first appeared, at times in somewhat different form:

Academy of American Poets (online): "Questions of Home"
Connect: Art, Politics, Theory, Practice: "Translating 'Passion'"
Crab Orchard Review: "Unquiet Borders"
Haritham: "Obstinate Questionings" (Under the title "Poetics of Dislocation")
Interventions: The International Journal of Postcolonial Studies (Inaugural Issue): "Rights of Passage"
Journal of Commonwealth Literature: "Poetry of Decreation"
Meridians: Feminism, Race, Transnationalism (Inaugural Issue): "'The Shock of Sensation': On Reading *The Waves* as a girl in India and a woman in North America"
n.paradoxa: http://www.nparadoxa.com: "This is not Me!"
Open Democracy http://www.opendemocracy.com: "Words in the Wind"
PEN America: "Silenced Writer"
Transformations: "Intimate Violence"
Triquarterly: "Encountering Emily" and "From 'Fragile Places: A Poet's Notebook'"
Virginia Quarterly Review (Special Issue on Walt Whitman): "In Whitman's Country"
Women's Review of Books: "Crossing Sabermati" (portion of "Fragile Places")

"Mortal Tracks" appeared as the catalogue essay for the show
"Rummana Hussein: In Order to Join" at Art in General,
New York City, October 1998

Under the title "Psychic Graffiti" the third section of the essay I have
titled "Composition" was published in *Performing Hybridities*, edited by
May Joseph and Jennifer Fink (University of Minnesota Press, 1999).
Under the title "Listening to Lorca" the fourth section of this same
essay was published in the Festival Catalogue, Poetry International
2002, Royal Festival Hall, London, June 2002.

Under the title "Writing Space" the lyric essay in several parts I have
called "Poetics of Dislocation" was published in the inaugural issue of
Contemporary Women's Writing (Inaugural Issue).
"Threshold City" in Italian translation was published together with
an interview by Daniela Ciani Forza in *Quale America? Soglie e culture
di un continente* Vol. 2 (Venezia: Mazzanti Editori, 2007)

The conversation with Ruth Maxey was first published in the *Kenyon
Review*.
The conversation with Roshni Rustomji-Kerns is published in *Passage
to Manhattan: Essays on Meena Alexander*, edited by Lopamudra Basu
and Cynthia Leenerts (Newcastle: Cambridge Scholars Publishing,
2009)

I would like to thank friends too numerous to name who over
the years have read these prose pieces. At CUNY Graduate Center my thanks to Lopamudra Basu, Geoffrey Jacques, Ronaldo
Wilson, Mahwash Shoiab, Richard Perez, and Maureen Fadem
with whom I have discussed poetics; to students who partici-
pated in the "Poetics of Dislocation" seminar; to my friend and
colleague Wayne Koestenbaum. My thanks to Fahmida Riaz in
Lahore; Paul Zachariah in Thiruvananthapuram for permission
to use our email conversations; thanks to Annie Finch and Mar-
ilyn Hacker, series editors. My gratitude to Gauri Viswanathan
for our close friendship over the years; to my family—David
Lelyveld, our son Adam Kuruvilla, our daughter Svati Mariam,
my loving thanks—you have sustained these reflections in ways
you will never know.

UNDER DISCUSSION
Annie Finch and Marilyn Hacker, General Editors
Donald Hall, Founding Editor

Volumes in the Under Discussion series collect reviews and essays about individual poets. The series is concerned with contemporary American and English poets about whom the consensus has not yet been formed and the final vote has not been taken. Titles in the series include: